COMPREHENSION SKILLS & STRATEGIES

in a Balanced Reading Program

by Dorothy Rubin, Ph.D.
The College of New Jersey

Fearon Teacher Aids
A Division of Frank Schaffer Publications, Inc.

Holstrom

Dedication

With love to my supportive and understanding
husband, Artie,
my precious daughters, Carol and Sharon,
my delightful grandchildren, Jennifer,
Andrew, Melissa, and Kelsey,
and my considerate and charming son-in-law, Seth.

Senior Editor: Kristin Eclov
Editor: Lisa Schwimmer Marier
Copyeditor: Janet Barker
Cover and Interior Design: RedLane Studio
Cover Illustration: Jack Lindstrom, FAB Artists
Illustration: Ray Barton

Fearon Teacher Aids products were formerly manufactured and distributed by American Teaching Aids, Inc., a subsidiary of Silver Burdett Ginn, and are now manufactured and distributed by Frank Schaffer Publications, Inc. FEARON, FEARON TEACHER AIDS, and the FEARON balloon logo are marks used under license from Simon & Schuster, Inc.

© **Fearon Teacher Aids**
A Division of Frank Schaffer Publications, Inc.
23740 Hawthorne Boulevard
Torrance, CA 90505-5927

© 1998 Fearon Teacher Aids. All rights reserved. Printed in the United States of America. This publication, or parts thereof, may not be reproduced in any form by photographic, electronic, mechanical, or any other method, for any use, including information storage and retrieval, without written permission from the publisher. Student reproducibles excepted.

FE7965
ISBN 0-7682-0043-1

Contents

About This Resource 6
    Whom This Guide Is For 6
    The Organization 7
    Some Suggestions for Use 8

What Is a Balanced Reading Program 9
    What Is the Role of the Teacher in a Balanced Reading Program? 9
    Scenario: Ms. Hall in Action 9

Strategies to Help Children Build Their Comprehension Ability 13
    Interactive Instruction 13
    Modeling Instruction 13
        Scenario: Ms. Hall Uses a Modeling Strategy with Her First-Graders 14
    Directed Reading Lesson Plan 15
    Checklist of Reading Comprehension Instruction 16
    Questioning Strategies to Enhance Comprehension Ability 17

Developing Selected Reading and Thinking Skills 19

Skill 1: Finding Details That Are Directly Stated 21
    Explanation 21
    Teaching Strategies in Action 21
        Sample Practices 21
        Modeling Strategy 22
    Learning Objective 23
    Directions for Student Practices 23
    Extensions 23
    Assessment Tool Progress Report 24
    Student Practices 25

Skill 2: Drawing Inferences—"Reading Between the Lines" 30
    Explanation 30
    Teaching Strategies in Action 31
        Sample Practices 32
        Modeling Strategy 32
    Learning Objective 33
    Directions for Student Practices 33
    Extensions 33
    Assessment Tool Progress Report 35
    Student Practices 36

Skill 3: Cause and Effect 46
    Explanation 46
    Teaching Strategies in Action 46
        Sample Practices 46
        Modeling Strategy 47
    Learning Objective 48
    Directions for Student Practices 48
    Extensions 49
    Assessment Tool Progress Report 50
    Student Practices 51

Skill 4: Finding the Main Idea of a Paragraph 56
    Explanation 56
    Teaching Strategies in Action 56
        Sample Practices 57
        Modeling Strategy 58
    Learning Objective 59
    Directions for Student Practices 59
    Extensions 60
    Assessment Tool Progress Report 61
    Student Practices 62

© Fearon Teacher Aids FE7965

Contents

Skill 5: Finding the Central Idea of a Story 67
    Explanation 67
    Teaching Strategies in Action 67
        Sample Practices 68
        Modeling Strategy 69
    Learning Objective 70
    Directions for Student Practices 70
    Extensions 70
    Assessment Tool Progress Report 72
    Student Practices 73

Skill 6: Following Directions 78
    Explanation 78
    Teaching Strategies in Action 78
        Sample Practices 79
        Modeling Strategy 80
    Learning Objective 80
    Directions for Student Practices 81
    Extensions 81
    Assessment Tool Progress Report 82
    Student Practices 83

Skill 7: Categorizing 93
    Explanation 93
    Teaching Strategies in Action 93
        Sample Practices 93
        Modeling Strategy 94
    Learning Objective 95
    Directions for Student Practices 95
    Extensions 95
    Assessment Tool Progress Report 97
    Student Practices 98

Skill 8: Completing Word Relationships (Analogies) 118
    Explanation 118
    Teaching Strategies in Action 118
        Sample Practices 119
        Modeling Strategy 119
    Learning Objective 122
    Directions for Student Practices 122
    Extensions 123
    Assessment Tool Progress Report 124
    Student Practices 125

Skill 9: Finding Inconsistencies 140
    Explanation 140
    Teaching Strategies in Action 140
        Sample Practices 140
        Modeling Strategy 141
    Learning Objective 141
    Directions for Student Practices 141
    Extensions 142
    Assessment Tool Progress Report 143
    Student Practices 144

Skill 10: Distinguishing Between Fact and Opinion 149
    Explanation 149
    Teaching Strategies in Action 149
        Sample Practices 149
        Modeling Strategy 150
    Learning Objective 150
    Directions for Student Practices 150
    Extensions 151
    Assessment Tool Progress Report 152
    Student Practices 153

Contents

Skill 11: Using Divergent Thinking 158
    Explanation 158
    Teaching Strategies in Action 158
        Sample Practices 159
        Modeling Strategy 159
    Learning Objective 160
    Directions for Student Practices 160
    Extensions 161
    Assessment Tool Progress Report 162
    Student Practices 163

Diagnostic Checklist for Selected Reading Comprehension Skills 168

Answers 169

About This Resource

Comprehension Skills and Strategies in a Balanced Reading Program is intended to be a valuable resource for parents and the classroom teacher by providing a wealth of challenging and stimulating reading comprehension activities for young students. The wide variety of material found in this resource will help parents and classroom teachers as they work with students of all ability levels. *Comprehension Skills and Strategies in a Balanced Reading Program* is published in a format that includes practice pages that are easily reproducible for distribution to children in classrooms or at home—an important time-saver for busy parents and teachers.

The skills and strategies presented in *Comprehension Skills and Strategies in a Balanced Reading Program* deal with reasoning with verbal concepts and word meanings—these are the two major abilities that are the basis for solid reading comprehension. Comprehension involves thinking. As there are various levels in the hierarchy of thinking, so are there various levels of reading comprehension. Higher levels of comprehension would obviously include higher levels of thinking. This book concentrates on the higher-order comprehension skills because these are the strategies often neglected in schools—and all students need help in acquiring these abilities. More and more across the country, teachers are emphasizing the teaching of higher-order comprehension skills and strategies.

This book is based on the premise that primary-grade children can and should be exposed to high-level comprehension skills at their individual literacy levels. As noted educator Jerome Bruner said in his book *The Process of Education* (Cambridge, MA: Harvard University Press, 1963), "Any subject can be taught effectively in some intellectually honest form to any child at any stage of development." While Bruner contends that this is a bold statement, there is little evidence to contradict it—and there is considerable evidence to support it. In the primary grades, children should be learning comprehension skills and strategies concomitantly with decoding, and these skills should be presented in a meaningful context. The material that the children are reading should be interesting and related as closely as possible to what the children are learning. Reading is a thinking act, and unless children comprehend what they are reading, they are not *really* reading.

Whom This Guide Is For

The material in *Comprehension Skills and Strategies in a Balanced Reading Program* is designed for students in the primary grades (K–3), but can be used with older students as well. The emphasis in this resource is on engaging children in activities that will help them become good, strategic readers.

Recent studies suggest strongly that "reading skill may not be developed as quickly or as well in the primary grades as is believed," and that "we are just beginning to detect the dire consequences that a poor initial start with reading has on later development." (From Connie Juel's "Beginning Reading," in *Handbook of Reading Research*, Vol. ll, Rebecca Barr, Michael L. Kamil, Peter Mosenthal, and P. David Pearson, eds. New York: Longman, 1991, p. 759.) *Comprehension Skills and Strategies in a Balanced Reading Program* can help ensure primary-grade teachers that students are learning the comprehension skills and strategies they need to become good readers and ultimately succeed in school.

If you are a teacher or parent with highly able children, you will find *Comprehension Skills and Strategies in a Balanced Reading Program* a helpful teaching tool as well. The material provides the kind of challenges in higher-order thinking that gifted children need and enjoy.

Each book in this series helps raise students test scores in a variety of areas. It can help students improve their scores on standardized achievement and basic skills tests, as well as on teacher-generated tests.

Comprehension Skills and Strategies in a Balanced Reading Program, as well as, *Vocabulary Skills and Strategies in a Balanced Reading Program* and the *Phonics: Skills and Strategies in a Balanced Reading Program* series helps students achieve better in school in all subject-matter areas. All of these books also start students on the road to preparing for the Scholastic Assessment Test (SAT).

The Organization

Comprehension Skills and Strategies in a Balanced Reading Program contains eleven skill areas for a total of 90 practice exercises. Each skill area includes accompanying teaching material and student practice sheets. The teaching material precedes the practices and contains the following:

Explanation
Teaching Strategies in Action
Sample Practices
Modeling Strategy
Learning Objective
Directions for Student Practices
Extensions
Assessment Tool Progress Report

The extensions in the teaching materials are intended to extend learning in each of the skill areas. Feel free to use some or all of them as is appropriate for your students.

The Assessment Tool Progress Report, as well as the practice exercises, are reproducible. The teaching material offers suggestions for record keeping and can be especially helpful for student portfolios.

The student practices for each skill are graduated in levels of difficulty. The beginning exercises are easier, the following are more difficult. You can, therefore, choose appropriate exercises based on the ability level of each student. The progression from easier to more difficult allows each student initial success in working with the material. Clear and understandable directions are provided for each exercise. For some of the exercises, when necessary, special teaching instructions are provided.

Some Suggestions for Use

Comprehension Skills and Strategies in a Balanced Reading Program can be used in various settings and with a variety of students. Regardless of the program you currently embrace, *Comprehension Skills and Strategies in a Balanced Reading Program* can help you stay aware of your students' individual differences as you continue to learn more about their reading behaviors.

I encourage you to continuously assess your children's reading behavior. You can gain information about your students' reading behavior using observation and student portfolios, as well as, when appropriate, informal and formal diagnostic measures. You then can use this data to either reinforce, supplement, enrich, or develop skill and strategy areas using material from *Comprehension Skills and Strategies in a Balanced Reading Program*.

The materials in this book can be used in working with individual children, in small groups, or with an entire class.

What Is a Balanced Reading Program?

A balanced reading program is one in which the best of whole language practices and a sequential development of skills are fully integrated. In such a program, teachers and parents integrate various aspects of the best of the whole language movement with different programs to achieve a balanced, eclectic approach that is also practical.

In a balanced reading program, the emphasis is on helping students improve their higher-order thinking skills, as well as gain needed comprehension and word recognition skills and strategies. In such a program, teachers also nurture a love of books in their students to help them become lifelong readers.

What Is the Role of the Teacher in a Balanced Reading Program?

Teachers are the key to the success of any program. Good teachers are aware of the individual differences of students in their classrooms, the interrelatedness of reading with the other language arts, and they understand their role in the teaching of reading.

In a balanced reading program, you, the teacher, are the key decision-maker. You determine which materials, practices, skills, and strategies to use based on the individual needs of your children. In a balanced reading program, teachers use trade books, children's writings, newspapers, textbooks, and all other appropriate materials as springboards for children's listening, speaking, reading, writing, and viewing.

Scenario: Ms. Hall in Action

Ms. Hall has been teaching reading to young children for over 30 years. She started teaching right out of college and prides herself on keeping abreast of her field. She especially enjoys noticing new trends and comparing them to the approaches she has used in her teaching over the years.

Ms. Hall loves to teach. This is evident in her relationships with her students and by what takes place in her classroom. When you ask Ms. Hall what excites her about teaching, she says, "Nothing can outdo the joy of knowing that you have taken children by the hand and helped them unlock the mystery of reading. What can be more exciting than seeing veiled eyes suddenly sparkle with a gleam that says 'I understand'? How many other careers are there that can bring such rewards each day?"

Ms. Hall has a group of 25 first-graders in her classroom. She is fortunate to have a teacher's aide with whom she works very closely. At the beginning of every year, Ms. Hall spends the first few weeks getting to know her students and establishing a non-threatening environment in her classroom where creativity can flourish and students are not afraid to be risk-takers.

During the first few weeks of school, Ms. Hall helps her students establish certain routines and procedures so they can live together in harmony. She encourages suggestions from the children. She also trains her teacher's aide to be more than an assistant. She helps her teacher's aide gain the strategies and skills she needs to help with direct instruction.

Ms. Hall engages her students in many activities in an attempt to gain as much information about her students as she can gather. She also establishes a classroom portfolio system where each child has a folder and in this folder the child stores samples of his or her work-in-progress.

Ms. Hall combines the data from her students' folders with observation and informal and formal tests to organize a program for her students. She knows all her students need to have many, many opportunities to read and write, positive feedback, direct instruction based on their needs, encouragement, and lots of on-task activities. During the school day, Ms. Hall works with the whole class, with individual children, and with small groups of students.

Ms. Hall uses a combination of soft-cover trade books and other reading materials and various approaches to help her students get the most from their reading. Whether she is using a basal reader or a trade book, she employs a directed or guided reading and thinking activity. She also uses the children's experiences to develop language experience stories that they write and read together.

If you were to enter Ms. Hall's first-grade classroom a few months into the school year, you would be greatly impressed with her students' activities. Let's spend part of a day with Ms. Hall in her balanced reading program.

Ms. Hall begins each day with a special poem that she shares with the class. Today she is reading aloud Amy Lowell's poem, "City of Falling Leaves", because today is a windy fall day and leaves of all colors are falling to the ground. After she reads the poem, she engages the children in a lively discussion about autumn and falling leaves. Ms. Hall asks the children whether all trees lose their leaves in the fall. "When you go home today," she says, "check to see if there are any trees that still have their leaves. We'll talk about these tomorrow."

Just then, a child raises his hand and says that he has lived in another part of the world where trees do not lose their leaves in the fall. He also says that the weather where he used to live almost never changes. Ms. Hall goes to the globe and points to the country where Stephan once lived before he and his family came to the United States. Ms. Hall tells the children that she spoke to Stephan and his mother and that next week Stephan's mother will come to school to talk about Stephan's homeland.

Ms. Hall says, "Stephan and his mother are coming to school to talk about the country Stephan and his family once lived in. I thought it would be a good idea if we learned something about the country first, so I went to the library and took out some books that have stories about the country Stephan is from. Then we can come up with some questions to ask Stephan and his mother. What do you think it would be like to live in a country that almost always has the same weather? Would it change your life? We'll talk about the questions later today."

Ms. Hall next invites her students to help in the general planning of the day's activities. This is what the class schedule looks like:

Reading groups
Reading aloud to children
Writing stories
Fun with words
Math (working with money—setting up a grocery store)
Lunch
Writing stories
Social studies unit
Storytelling
Creative drama
Special activities
Television reviews

Ms. Hall thanks her students for their help. She then calls a group of students to an area of the room for a small-group instructional unit. (While Ms. Hall is working with the group of students, her teacher's aide is seated in another part of the room surrounded by the rest of the children. The teacher's aide is reading aloud to the other students. She encourages predictions about what she is reading and asks questions before, during, and after.)

Ms. Hall shows her small group of children a nest with a little cloth hen sitting inside it. Ms. Hall asks the children where they think they might find chickens. A discussion ensues about farms and the kinds of animals children would find there. Ms. Hall asks if the children know what a female chicken is called. When a child says, "A hen," Ms. Hall says, "Good," and prints the word *hen* on the chalkboard. She then has the children generate a number of words using the *en* word family. First, she has them change the initial consonant to form new words. Then she has them change the final consonant. Ms. Hall puts each new word in a sentence. Ms. Hall asks the children for some other word families they have worked with before.

Ms. Hall then prints the following words on the board:

flour	wheat
bread	grain
mill	plant

After Ms. Hall helps the children gain the vocabulary words, she helps them place each new word in a sentence. She then tells the children they will be reading a story about a little red hen who has three friends. Ms. Hall explains that at the end of the story, the children will find out what kind of friends the little red hen has.

As the children read, Ms. Hall observes the children's reading behavior. Each time the children finish reading a section silently, she asks them to answer some questions. For example, Ms. Hall asks the children what they think the little red hen will do with the wheat. She asks why the little red hen's wheat grew so well. Then she asks the children to find the clues in the story that help them answer these questions and to read the clues aloud.

Throughout the story, Ms. Hall sets purposes for the silent and oral reading and has children make predictions about what they are reading. Before the children come to the end of the story, Ms. Hall asks the children to think about how they would end the story. She writes the children's predictions on paper. Ms. Hall then has the children read the final page in the book to find out what really happens. She then has the children compare their endings with the story's ending. The amount of time Ms. Hall spends on this lesson is based on the attention span and ability levels of the children.

After all the children have returned to their seats, Ms. Hall and the teacher's aide play a game of "Simon Says" with the children. They have a short recess and then Ms. Hall calls the next group to the reading table while the teacher's aide reads aloud to the other group.

Strategies to Help Children Build Their Comprehension Ability

The emphasis in this book is on providing direct instruction to the children. *Direct instruction* is instruction guided by a teacher who uses various strategies or techniques to help children comprehend what they are reading. There are a number of strategies you can use to teach reading directly. The strategies that you use should not be affected by the kinds of materials you use. In other words, one teacher may use only trade books in his or her class, while another might use a basal reader. Both teachers can employ similar strategies to help students gain needed concepts. As stated previously, this text advocates a mix of materials, beliefs, and strategies.

> **Special Note**
>
> A *strategy* is a systematic plan for achieving a specific objective or result. An *instructional reading strategy* is the action or actions that a teacher takes to help children gain reading skills.

Interactive Instruction

In interactive instruction, the teacher intervenes at optimal times to improve classroom instruction. The teacher determines when to intervene and what materials and strategies to use to achieve the desired learning for the readers with whom she or he is working.

Modeling Instruction

Modeling instruction requires teachers to think out loud. That is, teachers verbalize their thoughts to help students "see" an appropriate strategy or reading behavior. This is an exceptionally effective strategy because it helps students gain insight into the kind of thinking involved in reading comprehension and helps children recognize that reading comprehension is analogous to problem solving.

Interactive instruction combined with modeling and knowledge of questioning techniques at various levels is very effective in helping students find meaning in what they are reading.

Scenario: Ms. Hall Uses a Modeling Strategy with Her First-Graders

Ms. Hall and seven children are working together at the reading table. They have been reading the story, "The Hare and the Tortoise." Ms. Hall has discussed with the children what a hare and a tortoise are. She has shown the children pictures of both and talked about which animal they would expect to move faster and why. She has gone over all new or unfamiliar words in the story with the children, and before they began to read the story, she had asked the children to make predictions about who they thought would win the race.

Today Ms. Hall has asked the children to do something a little different. They are going to be detectives. After discussing what a detective does, Ms. Hall asks the children to look for clues in the story to show why the hare lost the race.

She rereads the story with the children before she shows them how to find story clues. Then she says, "While I am reading the first two pages of the story, I see something that tells me the rabbit is very sure of himself. I think to myself that this will probably get him into trouble. Hare said, 'Rabbits run fast as the wind.' I don't think he took Tortoise very seriously. Hare feels it's silly to think that Tortoise could possibly win. Because of this, Hare feels he can take it easy. Now, everyone look at the next page. Are there any clues there that show us that the hare could lose the race?"

Ms. Hall calls on different children and elicits from them the reasons for their choices. When they have finished giving all their clues, Ms. Hall asks the children if they have ever heard the saying, "Slow and steady wins the race." She asks the children to think about what this means. Later, she says, they will discuss this.

On the following two pages, you will find an outline for a directed reading lesson plan, as well as a checklist, to use when preparing a reading program. Feel free to use these to help you in organizing your reading lesson plan.

Directed Reading Lesson Plan

Lesson plans usually vary based on grade level, whether it is a follow-up lesson, or whether it is at the beginning of a unit or theme. At the kindergarten level, the lessons often are listening lessons. At the beginning of first grade, there will be more reading aloud than silent reading to ensure that children are able to identify the words. The amount of time for lessons will vary based on the attention span of students, grade level, and number of groups. Make sure that each lesson includes comprehension questions and that you do not spend the whole lesson only on word recognition.

Objectives for Lesson

Step I: Preparing for Reading

Present motivating technique(s).

Relate to students' past experiences.

Use modeling strategy to develop skill necessary for reading lesson (skill should be related to what students are reading).

Present vocabulary words needed for lesson (words should be presented in context).

Tell students what they will be doing.

Step II: Silent and Oral Reading

Using title of story or chapter, have students make predictions about what they are going to read.

Have students read to answer questions (construct questions at the literal, interpretive, critical, and creative levels).

Have students answer questions in own words.

Then have students behave like detectives and have them read aloud the clues in the text that helped them answer the questions.

Step III: Summary

Help children pull main points of lesson together.

Step IV: Preparation for Student Work

Have worksheet that reinforces lesson—useful for diagnostic purposes.

Clearly explain written and reading assignments.

Make sure students know what to do after they have finished their assignments.

Step V: Extensions

Relate lesson to other language arts, math, science, social studies, art, and other areas.

Checklist of Reading Comprehension Instruction

Here is a checklist that you can use when preparing a reading lesson to determine whether you are using techniques that will help ensure that your students are actively engaged in learning.

Be sure to:

1. relate reading material to students' background knowledge.
2. have students make predictions about material to be read.
3. ask questions before reading.
4. ask questions during reading.
5. ask questions at the end of reading.
6. encourage students to ask questions about the material.
7. ask interpretive questions.
8. ask critical-thinking questions.
9. ask creative-thinking questions.
10. have students verify predictions.
11. have students find evidence from material to support their answers.
12. use visual representations to show relationships of main plot to subplots.
13. ask students to summarize the material.
14. model (think aloud) the steps you go through to gain understanding.
15. know when to intervene to benefit comprehension.

Questioning Strategies to Enhance Comprehension Ability

All children need help in developing higher-order reading comprehension ability. And asking only literal-type comprehension questions that demand a simple convergent answer won't develop these important higher-order skills.

Much of what has gone on in the past in our schools has been at the literal comprehension level. Teachers in the past often asked questions that required only a literal response. This started to change when the teaching of higher-order comprehension skills was encouraged.

Rather than ask a question that calls for a literal response, more and more teachers are learning to ask questions that call for higher levels of thinking—even as early as kindergarten and first grade. For example, the children have looked at a picture in which children are dressed in snow pants, jackets, hats, mittens, and so on. The teacher can then ask the following questions:

1. What kind of a day is it?
2. Where are the children going?

As children progress to higher levels of thinking, they should be confronted with more complex interpretation or inference problems—according to their individual developmental levels.

Critical reading skills are essential to being a good reader. Teachers can use primary graders' love of fairy tales to begin to develop some critical reading skills. For example, after the children have read, "Little Red Riding Hood," ask questions like the following:

1. Should Little Red Riding Hood have listened to her mother and not spoken to a stranger? Explain.
2. Would you help a stranger if your mother told you not to speak to a stranger? Explain.
3. Do you think a wolf can talk? Explain.
4. Do you think that this story is true? Explain.
5. Do you think Little Red Riding Hood made wise choices? Explain.

Creative reading questions are probably the most difficult for teachers to come up with. To help children in this area, teachers need to learn how to ask questions that require divergent rather than convergent answers. A teacher who focuses only on the author's meaning or intent and does not go beyond the text will not be encouraging creative reading. Questions that stimulate the reader's divergent thinking follow:

1. After reading "Little Red Riding Hood," can you come up with another ending for the story?
2. After reading about John, can you come up with a plan for the kind of vacation he would like?
3. After reading the story about the cat that escaped from the well, can you come up with some ideas as to how he was able to escape?
4. Based on your reading about John and his family, what kind of trip would you plan to make them happy?

With divergent questions, there is no one correct answer.

The following is a short reading selection and examples of four different types of comprehension questions. Practice recognizing the different types of questions at the four different levels.

One day in the summer, some of my friends and I decided to go on an overnight hiking trip. We all started out fresh and full of energy. About halfway to our destination, when the sun was almost directly overhead, one-third of my friends decided to return home. The remaining four of us, however, continued on our hike. Our plan was to reach our destination by sunset. About six hours later, as the four of us, exhausted and famished, were slowly edging ourselves in the direction of the setting sun, we saw a sight that astonished us. There, at the camping site, were our friends who had claimed that they were returning home. It seems that they did indeed go home, but only to pick up a car and drive out to the campsite.

The following are four different types of comprehension questions:

Literal comprehension: What season of the year was it in the story?

Interpretation: About what time of day was it when some of the hikers decided to return home? How many hikers were there when they first started out on the trip? In what direction were the hikers heading when they saw a sight that astonished them? At approximately what time did the sun set? How long did it take for the hikers to reach their destination?

Critical reading: How do you think the hikers felt when they reached their destination? Do you feel that the hikers who went home did the right thing by driving back to the site rather than hiking? Explain.

Creative reading: What do you think the exhausted hikers did and said when they saw their friends who had supposedly gone home?

Developing Selected Reading and Thinking Skills

Reading comprehension is a complex intellectual process involving a number of abilities. The two major abilities, as already stated, have to do with reasoning with verbal concepts and word meanings. Obviously, comprehension involves thinking. Asking only comprehension questions of a literal type, which demand a simple convergent answer that is explicitly stated in the text, does not contribute to the development of higher-order thinking skills. In this book, the emphasis is mainly on practices that require a higher level of thinking.

At the beginning of the book, some literal comprehension questions are included, because the literal comprehension questions are the easiest to answer. These have been presented at the beginning of the book to ensure the child of some success. The literal comprehension questions are followed by interpretive-type questions and those requiring critical and divergent thinking.

The critical and divergent thinking skills, which are high-level skills, are usually presented to older or more experienced students—sometimes they are not presented at all. In this book, the critical and divergent thinking skills are being presented because students should be encouraged to engage in these types of thinking as early in their school careers as possible.

Feel free to change the order to any sequence that you feel will better suit the needs of your individual students.

The exercises in this book concern reading and thinking skills that require reasoning with verbal concepts. A brief explanation of the selected reading and thinking skills presented in the section follows.

Skill 1	Finding Details That Are Directly Stated	To find information that is directly stated; information that is based on recall.
Skill 2	Drawing Inferences—"Reading Between the Lines"	To gain understanding from information that is not directly stated.
Skill 3	Cause and Effect	To determine what makes something happen—that is why it happens (cause) and the result (effect).

Skill 4	Finding the Main Idea of a Paragraph	To supply the main thought of a paragraph by determining what the topic is and what is special about the topic. All sentences in the paragraph should develop the main idea.
Skill 5	Finding the Central Idea of a Story	To supply the central thought of a group of paragraphs or a story by determining what the topic is and what is special about the topic. All paragraphs should develop the central idea.
Skill 6	Following Directions	To read instructions and then carry them out.
Skill 7	Categorizing	To classify items into a more general group or to determine whether an item belongs in a specific group.
Skill 8	Completing Word Relationships (Analogies)	To discern relationships between words or ideas.
Skill 9	Finding Inconsistencies	To supply the correct word by drawing a logical conclusion from a sentence or story material.
Skill 10	Distinguishing Between Fact and Opinion	To differentiate between information that can be verified and information that cannot be proven.
Skill 11	Using Divergent Thinking	To go beyond what the author has written to come up with new or alternate solutions.

Skill 1: Finding Details That Are Directly Stated

Explanation

Finding details that are directly stated in a story involves finding information that is clearly expressed within the story. It is a literal comprehension skill that is based on the students' recall of the facts in the story.

Finding details that are directly stated is an activity in which children usually do well. Though children generally have little difficulty with literal comprehension skills, they should certainly have practice with them. In order for children to be able to work with inference (see page 30, Skill 2), they need to first learn to recognize the difference between information that is directly stated and information that is not directly stated.

Teaching Strategies in Action

Children need to learn that some information is directly stated in a story and some information is not. Teachers can model for the children how they go about finding information that is directly stated.

Example:
"Miguel and Jackie went to the store."

In this sentence, the details are directly stated—both Miguel and Jackie went to the store. Children do not have to guess what is going on in the sentence because the details are directly stated.

Sample Practices

Here are some sample practices that you can use with your students:

1. Janel and Annette had eggs and toast for breakfast.

Question:
What did Janel and Annette have for breakfast?
Answer:
They had eggs and toast for breakfast.

2. Darnell and Rusty were playing pinball. Darnell got more points at the end of the game than Rusty. Darnell won the game.

Question:
What were Darnell and Rusty playing?
Answer:
They were playing pinball.

Question:
Who won the game?
Answer:
Darnell won the game.

Help your students understand that they can get the information they need by reading it in the text. The answers are directly stated in the story.

Modeling Strategy

Here is how Mr. Johnson models for the children how to find information that is directly stated for the following short selection and the questions that follow it.

Lisa has a pretty little white cat named Snowflake. Lisa likes to play with Snowflake. Snowflake drinks milk from a saucer. Lisa takes good care of Snowflake and Snowflake is happy to be Lisa's pet.

Questions:
1. Who has a cat?
2. What size is the cat?
3. What is the cat's name?
4. What color is the cat?
5. What does the cat drink?
6. Out of what does the cat drink?
7. How does the cat feel about being a pet?

Mr. Johnson asks his students to first read the passage. He says he will also read the passage. Mr. Johnson reads aloud the first question. Then he says, "I remember that the first sentence says that Lisa has a pretty little white cat named Snowflake. The short story tells me the answer. It is right there in the first sentence. Now, I read the second question. Again, I remember that the answer is right there in the story. It is directly stated. I can go to the story and find the answer." Mr. Johnson does just that. After he answers the question, he goes to the story and reads aloud the answer. Mr. Johnson does the same for another question. He helps his students see that the answer is directly stated in the story.

After Mr. Johnson has modeled for his students how he answers the questions, he has the students answer the rest of the questions. Mr. Johnson has the children answer the questions based on what the children remember and then find the answer in the story. When they have found the answer, he has one child read the answer aloud.

Learning Objective

To find information that is directly stated in a passage or story.

Directions for Student Practices

Use the student practice worksheets on pages 25–29 to help your students acquire, reinforce, and review finding details directly stated in the text. Pick and choose the practices based on the needs and developmental levels of your students. Answers for the student practice pages are on page 169.

When practicing finding details directly stated in the text, have the children read the story and then answer the questions. For those who have difficulty reading, read the story aloud to the children and orally ask them the questions.

Extensions

Picture Postcards
Invite children to create picture postcards. Give each child a large index card and encourage them to use their imaginations to draw and color the postcards. The postcards can be from Zip and Zap on the moon or the children can write their own postcards to family and friends from the moon, another country, or anywhere else they wish.

Puppets
Invite children to make stick puppets of each of the characters in a favorite story. Then challenge children to use their puppets to act out a scene or tell the class about their character.

Asking Questions
After reading a story together or in small groups, divide the class into pairs and invite children to take turns asking each other questions about the story.

Write a Poem
Review with the children the main characters, setting, and plot of a story. Then invite students to write poems about the story, keeping in mind the important details.

What Would You Like to Know?
Encourage students to write four or five questions they would like to ask the main characters of a favorite story. For more of a challenge, ask students to switch papers with another person and invite students to pretend they are one of the main characters in the story and answer their partners' questions.

Skill 1: Finding Details That Are Directly Stated

Student's Name _____

Assessment Tool Progress Report

Progress

Improvement

Comments

Skill 1: Finding Details That Are Directly Stated

Name _____

Practice 1

This is a make-believe story about an imaginary cat and rat who live on the moon.

Zip is a cat that lives on the moon. Zip has a friend named Zap. Zap is a rat. On the moon, cats and rats play together. They have lots of fun.

1. What is the name of the cat?

   _____

2. What is the name of the rat?

   _____

3. Where do Zip and Zap live?

   _____

4. What do they do together on the moon?

   _____

5. What friends play together on the moon?

   _____

Skill 1: Finding Details That Are Directly Stated

Name _____

Practice 2

This is a make-believe story about an imaginary cat and rat who live on the moon.

Zip, the cat, and Zap, the rat, live together. All the cats and rats on the moon live together. They live in one very large house. This house is filled with air. Zip and Zap like to go outside. They have to wear special air masks when they go outside. Zip and Zap laugh when they see how they look in their air masks.

1. Who lives together?

   _____

2. What kind of a house do Zip and Zap live in?

   _____

3. What do Zip and Zap have to wear when they go outside?

   _____

4. What does Zip and Zap's house have inside that is not outside?

   _____

5. What do Zip and Zap do when they see themselves in their air masks?

   _____

© Fearon Teacher Aids FE7965
Reproducible

Skill 1: Finding Details That Are Directly Stated

Name _____

Practice 3

This is a make-believe story about an imaginary cat and rat who live on the moon.

Zip and Zap were very happy. They were going to visit their Earth cousins. They talked about nothing else on their trip. As soon as daylight came, they would go on their trip. The space shuttle was going to take them to Earth. Zip and Zap had never been in the space shuttle. They had never been off the moon. This would be an adventure for them.

1. How did Zip and Zap feel?

   _____

2. When would Zip and Zap go on their trip?

   _____

3. Whom were Zip and Zap going to visit?

   _____

4. How were Zip and Zap going to get to Earth?

   _____

5. Have Zip and Zap ever been off the moon?

   _____

© Fearon Teacher Aids FE7965
Reproducible

Skill 1: Finding Details That Are Directly Stated

Name _____

Practice 4

This is a make-believe story about an imaginary cat and rat who live on the moon.

Zip and Zap went to the library to take out books about the Earth. They also wanted to see some pictures of the Earth. Zip and Zap walked to the middle of the large house where the library was. They went into the brightly lit room. The room was round and filled with other rats and cats. Zip and Zap went to the letter **E** and found the word **Earth**. They pressed a button and out came lots of books on the planet Earth. Zip and Zap pressed another button. This time, a large screen came out of the wall and the lights went out. Zip pressed another button. On the screen were pictures of the Earth. Zip and Zap watched the pictures and spent a long time in the library.

1. Where did Zip and Zap go?

   _____

2. What did Zip and Zap want?

   _____

3. Describe the library.

   _____

4. Where is the library located?

   _____

5. What books did Zip and Zap want?

   _____

6. What did Zip and Zap do to find the books they wanted?

   _____

7. What did Zip and Zap watch on the screen?

   _____

© Fearon Teacher Aids FE7965
Reproducible

Skill 1: Finding Details That Are Directly Stated

Name _____

Practice 5

This is a make-believe story about an imaginary cat and rat who live on the moon.

Zip and Zap were going to Earth. They put on their special clothing and their air masks. They got into the space shuttle and in a few moments, they zoomed off to Earth. Before Zip and Zap could say, "Hooray," they landed on Earth. Their Earth cousins were waiting for them. They looked so funny. They wore short pants and little shirts and they didn't wear any masks. The Earth cousins told Zip and Zap to take off their masks. They told Zip and Zap that they didn't need air masks on Earth. When they got to the Earth cousins' house, Zip and Zap put on the special Earth clothing. Zip and Zap looked at themselves in the mirror. They laughed.

1. What did Zip and Zap wear in the space shuttle?

   _____

2. How did Zip and Zap get to Earth?

   _____

3. Who were waiting for them when they arrived on Earth?

   _____

4. How did the Earth cousins look to Zip and Zap?

   _____

5. What weren't the Earth cousins wearing?

   _____

6. What did Zip and Zap not need on Earth?

   _____

7. What did Zip and Zap do when they got to their Earth cousins' house?

   _____

8. What did Zip and Zap do when they saw themselves in the mirror?

   _____

© Fearon Teacher Aids FE7965
Reproducible

Skill 2:
Drawing Inferences—"Reading Between the Lines"

Explanation

Writers often do not directly state what they mean, but present ideas in a more indirect, roundabout way. That is why inference is called the ability to "read between the lines." Inference is defined as "understanding that is not derived from a direct statement but from an indirect suggestion."

The ability to draw inferences is especially important in reading fiction, but it is also necessary when reading nonfiction. Authors rely on a reader's ability to infer meaning to make their stories more interesting and enjoyable. Mystery writers find inference essential to the suspense in their stories. For example, Sherlock Holmes and Perry Mason mysteries are based on the ability of the characters to uncover clues that are not obvious to others around them.

Question Answer Relationships (QARs) can be very useful in introducing children to inferential reasoning. This process can help children understand better what information is directly stated and what is implied. In the QAR technique, students learn that they not only must consider information that is in the text, but also information they already know. Here are some of the things that you can do to help children recognize the differences between information that is in the story and information that they already have in their heads—that is, information they bring to the story. Present children with a story, such as the following:

> Pete and his brother went to the ball game.
> They were lucky to get tickets for the game.
> They saw many people that they knew.
> At the game, Pete and his brother ate hot dogs.
> They also drank soda.

Then ask the children the following questions:

> 1. Where did Pete and his brother go? (To the ball game)
> 2. Where did they see the people? (At the ball game)

Help the children see that the first answer is directly stated in the passage. The first sentence says that Pete and his brother went to the ball game. The answer to the second sentence is not directly stated. The answer to the second question is already in the children's heads because they know from the first sentence that Pete and his brother went to the ball game. Therefore, the children can infer that Pete and his brother saw many people at the ball game from reading the first sentence.

Inference is an important process that authors rely on. Good readers must be alert to the ways that authors encourage inference.

Special Note

Interpretation questions concern answers that are not directly stated in the text but are implied. All questions at the interpretive level are inference questions. Because of this, there is generally confusion concerning the term *inference*. The definition of inference is very broad and includes all of the skills that come under the interpretive level. However, when teachers refer to inference, they are usually referring to the specific skill of "reading between the lines."

Teaching Strategies in Action

To understand text, the reader must be alert and able to detect the clues that the author gives.

Example:
Things are always popping and alive when the twins, Jason and Scott, are around.

In this sentence, you are given some clues to Jason and Scott's personalities, even though the author has not directly said anything about their personalities. From the statement, you could make the inference that the twins are lively and fun, or maybe even devious or troublesome.

Caution your students not to read more into statements than is intended. Read the following statement.

Example:
Mary got out of bed and looked out of the window. She saw that the ground had some white on it.

Question:
What season of the year was it?
Answer:
(a) winter; (b) summer; (c) spring; (d) fall; (e) can't tell.

The answer is "(e) can't tell." Many people choose "(a) winter" for the answer. However, the answer is (e) because the "something white" could be anything; there isn't enough evidence to choose (a). Even if the something white were snow, in some parts of the world, including the United States, it can snow in the spring or fall.

Sample Practices

Here are some sample practices that you can use with your students.

1. Mary looked out of the train window. She saw some leafless trees.

Question:
What season of the year was it? Circle the correct answer and give reasons for your answer.
(a) winter; (b) summer; (c) fall; (d) spring; (e) can't tell
Answer:
e) can't tell. It could be any season of the year. We do not know in which part of the country or world Mary is traveling. The trees could be leafless as a result of a forest fire, disease, or some other cause.

2. The hikers walked toward the mountain range. Some of the hikers needed to sit down. They were out of breath.

Question:
Why were the hikers out of breath?
Answer:
Because they were tired or because of the high altitude.

Help your students see that the clues are not directly stated in the story, but that they are all there.

Modeling Strategy

Ms. Stein writes a short paragraph with questions on the board. Here it is:

The horses had been out in the desert for a long time. Their manes were covered with dust. The sun beat down on them and they needed something to drink.

Questions:
1. What kind of a day was it?
2. Why did the horses need something to drink?

Ms. Stein says the following:

"Let's read the paragraph together. Now, I'm going to say aloud how I would answer the first question, 'What kind of a day was it?' See if you agree. I remember that the last line of the paragraph says that the sun beat down on them, so it must be hot. But I also see that the horses' manes were covered with dust. So it must be a very dry day. I infer or read between the lines that it is a very dry day. Now I read the second question, which is, 'Why did the horses need something to drink?' I remember that the horses are in the desert. A desert is usually dry. The last sentence starts with 'The sun beat down on them' so I know it's also hot. The horses are hot and dry which probably makes them thirsty. So I see that the answer to the second question is that the horses need something to drink because they are thirsty."

Ms. Stein then writes another paragraph on the board. Here it is:

The children were hiking toward a forest. The sun was setting behind the trees. When they got to the forest, the children decided to sit down and have a snack.

Question:
In what direction were the children going?

"Here's what I do to answer this question. First I think what clues help me figure out direction. Let's see, the children are walking toward the forest. The second sentence says the sun was setting behind the trees. I already know that the sun sets in the West. Because the sun is setting behind the trees, the children are going west."

Ms. Stein helps the children see that even though the clues are not directly stated in the story, there is enough information to answer the question.

Learning Objective

To draw inferences or "read between the lines" to find meaning.

Directions for Student Practices

Use the student practices on pages 36–45 to help your students acquire, reinforce, and review drawing inferences. Pick and choose the practices based on the needs and developmental levels of your students. Answers for the student practice pages are on pages 169–170.

When practicing drawing inferences, have the children read the story and then answer the questions. For those who have difficulty reading, read the story aloud to the children and ask them to respond to the questions orally.

Extensions

Characterization

Have each student choose a character from a favorite story and describe one thing about that character. Ask for explanations. Then invite each student to cover a box with paper. On one side, he or she can draw a picture of the chosen character. On the remaining sides of the box, he or she can give written or picture examples of actions in the story that describe the character.

Postcards and Letters

Encourage each student to write a postcard or letter to a character in a favorite story. Invite students to write about an experience that they had that was similar to something that happened in the story. Encourage children to share their postcards and letters with the class or display the postcards and letters in the classroom.

Making Dioramas

Invite children to create dioramas of the setting based on information given in a favorite story. Children can make a classroom diorama or you may want to divide the class into small groups and invite each group to make a diorama. Encourage children to display their dioramas as well as explain what is going on in each.

Living On the Moon

Invite children to write a story about what they think it would be like to live on the moon. Have them think about what kinds of foods they would eat on the moon. Ask children if there are any trees, what the Earth looks like from the moon, and so on. Encourage children to be creative.

Skill 2: Drawing Inferences—"Reading Between the Lines"

Student's Name _____

Assessment Tool Progress Report

Progress

Improvement

Comments

Skill 2: Drawing Inferences—"Reading Between the Lines"

Name _____

Practice 1

This is a make-believe story about an imaginary cat and rat who live on the moon.

Imagine that on the moon, all the food is grown inside a very large house. Zip and Zap, a cat and rat who live on the moon, like to watch the food grow. The food is grown inside the house because there is no air or water outside. The food is grown in a special place and in a special way. Zip and Zap use the same water that the first rats and cats brought to the moon many years ago.

1. Have the cats and the rats lived on the moon forever? Explain.

   _____

2. Why is water reused?

   _____

3. What are two things that are very precious on the moon?

   _____

4. What do plants need in order to grow?

   _____

© Fearon Teacher Aids FE7965
Reproducible

Skill 2: Drawing Inferences—"Reading Between the Lines"

Name _____

Practice 2

This is a make-believe story about an imaginary cat and rat who live on the moon.

Zip and Zap love to ride in space. Their school goes on a space trip every month. Zip and Zap wear their space clothes and their air masks in the spaceship. All the other moon cats and rats wear them, too. Zip and Zap want to be spaceship pilots. They want to pilot the same spaceship that brought Zip and Zap to the moon a few years ago. The spaceship has its own landing place. It is well taken care of by special cats and rats. Zip and Zap are happy that they can ride in the spaceship.

1. Is there air in the spaceship? Explain.

   _____

2. Were Zip and Zap born on the moon? Explain.

   _____

3. Is the spaceship important to the moon cats and rats? Explain.

   _____

4. Is travel an important part of school? Explain.

   _____

© Fearon Teacher Aids FE7965
Reproducible

Skill 2: Drawing Inferences—"Reading Between the Lines"

Name _____

Practice 3

This is a make-believe story about an imaginary cat and rat who live on the moon.

Zip, the cat, and Zap, the rat, wear special clothing on the moon. They must wear this special clothing whenever they go outside. If they did not wear the special clothing, they would not be able to breathe. They also might float away. One day, while they were playing tag inside, Zip was running after Zap. Zap ran outside and jumped up and down. Zip ran outside, too. Zip jumped up, but didn't come down. Zap turned around. When he did, he saw Zip floating away! "Oh, no!" screamed Zap. "Come back! Come back!" But Zip just floated away.

1. Who was wearing special outdoor clothing? How do you know?

   _____

2. Why did Zip float away?

   _____

3. What do you think happened to Zip?

   _____

4. Did Zip think carefully before he ran outside? Explain.

   _____

© Fearon Teacher Aids FE7965
Reproducible

Name _____

Practice 4

Directions: Read the make-believe story about Zip and Zap, an imaginary cat and rat who live on the moon. Write or state 5 things about the person or animal who saved Zip. Give clues from the story to support your thinking.

Zip knew that he was in trouble. He floated and floated higher and higher. When he looked down, he couldn't see Zap at all. Zip was frightened. Whenever Zip was frightened, he would close his eyes. All of a sudden, he felt something grab him. He opened his eyes, but he couldn't see anything. He knew that he had stopped floating, but he didn't know where he was. Just then he heard a booming voice. It was so loud that he thought his ears would burst. "Ho, ho, ho, a suitless wonder," the voice said. Zip heard the voice, but still couldn't see where it was coming from. "Well, you're safe now," said the voice. The next thing Zip knew, he was inside the door of his house. Zip was happy to be home. Zap was happy to have Zip home, too.

Skill 2: Drawing Inferences—"Reading Between the Lines"

Name _____

Practice 5

Directions: Read the make-believe story about Zip and Zap, an imaginary cat and rat who live on the moon. Then read each of the sentences below the story. For each of the sentences, see if there is enough information in the story to write **true** or **false**. If there is not enough information, write **can't tell**.

Zip and Zap go to school when it is dark outside. Darkness lasts for 14 Earth days. Daylight lasts for 14 Earth days, too. Zip and Zap do lots of things in school. They learn to read and write. They even have their own robot who helps them. The robot can answer any questions that Zip and Zap might have. They keep their robot busy. Zip and Zap enjoy learning about the Earth and other planets. They like school very much.

1. Zip and Zap go to school for 14 Earth days. _____

2. One moon day lasts for 28 Earth days. _____

3. Zip and Zap sleep for 14 days in a row. _____

4. Zip and Zap ask their robot lots of questions. _____

5. Zip and Zap do not want to go to school. _____

6. Zip and Zap have lots of tests in school. _____

7. Zip and Zap get good grades in school. _____

8. Zip and Zap's robot can do lots of things. _____

9. Zip and Zap are interested in geography. _____

10. Zip and Zap do not have a teacher. _____

Name _____

Practice 6

Directions: Read the story. Read each of the sentences below the story. For each of the sentences, see if there is enough information in the story to write **true** or **false**. If there is not enough information, write **can't tell**.

I would like to play outside today. My mother says I have to wear my snowsuit, hat, and mittens. I am going to build a fort and make a snowman. I see Lucy ice-skating on the pond. I want to play with her.

1. The person in the story is a boy. _____

2. There is snow on the ground. _____

3. It is cold outside. _____

4. The pond is frozen. _____

5. The person in the story wants to play alone. _____

Skill 2: Drawing Inferences—"Reading Between the Lines"

Name _____

Practice 7

Directions: Read the story. Then read each of the sentences below the story. For each of the sentences, see if there is enough information in the story to write **true** or **false**. If there is not enough information, write **can't tell**.

John and Jim became friends in kindergarten. When Jim came to school the first day, he was frightened and began to cry. John saw Jim crying. He said, "Come sit by me," and took Jim's hand. John led Jim to his table and Jim stopped crying. From then on, whenever you saw John, you would know that Jim was close by. The next year of school though, something happened. Whenever you saw John, Jim was not with him.

1. John and Jim are about the same age. _____

2. John and Jim have been friends for 10 years. _____

3. Jim likes broccoli. _____

4. John will be a leader when he grows up. _____

5. John and Jim had a fight. _____

6. Jim moved away. _____

7. John was kind to Jim in kindergarten. _____

8. John and Jim were close friends in kindergarten. _____

9. John and Jim have been friends for about four years. _____

10. John and Jim knew each other before kindergarten. _____

© Fearon Teacher Aids FE7965
Reproducible

Name _____

Practice 8

Directions: Read the story. Then read each of the sentences below the story. For each of the sentences, see if there is enough information in the story to write **true** or **false**. If there is not enough information, write **can't tell**.

The school picnic is tomorrow and all the children can hardly wait. The parents cooked and baked lots of things for the picnic. There are many games to play at the picnic and the teachers and parents play the games, too. Every year, the picnic begins when the sun is almost directly overhead. At the end of the picnic, everyone stands in front of the school building and watches the sun slowly set behind the school building. Then everyone slowly drags himself or herself home.

1. The children are excited about the school picnic. _____

2. Parents come to the school picnic. _____

3. At the end of the school picnic, everyone is tired. _____

4. The school picnic starts about noon. _____

5. The school picnic takes place on a school day. _____

6. The teachers play against parents in the games. _____

7. The front of the school building faces west. _____

8. Prizes are given out at the picnic. _____

9. If it rains, the picnic will be held on another day. _____

10. The picnic has always been held on a sunny day. _____

Skill 2: Drawing Inferences—"Reading Between the Lines"

Name _____

Practice 9

Directions: Read the story. Read each of the sentences below the story. For each of the sentences, see if there is enough information in the story to write **true** or **false**. If there is not enough information, write **can't tell**.

Three turtles were sitting on a log. The first turtle turned to the other two and said, "This is my log! You have to get off." The other two turtles looked at each other and slowly crawled onto another nearby log.

The two turtles spent the day sunning themselves and chatting about the weather. The first turtle sat all by himself with no other turtles to talk to. Soon the first turtle slowly made his way over to the other two turtles. He crawled up beside them on their new log and sat quietly. The other two turtles turned to him and said, "Welcome! Would you like to sun yourself with us on our log?" The first turtle said, "Yes, thank you." The three turtles spent the rest of the day sunning themselves and chatting about the weather.

1. This is a true story.   _____

2. It was a sunny day.   _____

3. The first turtle liked to share.   _____

4. The first turtle got lonely.   _____

5. All three turtles were males.   _____

6. The turtles were all very old.   _____

7. The two other turtles were kind.   _____

8. It is springtime in the story.   _____

© Fearon Teacher Aids FE7965
Reproducible

Skill 2: Drawing Inferences—"Reading Between the Lines"

Name _____

Practice 10

Directions: Read the story. Then answer the questions that follow the story.

Once there was a rich and wise man. He had become rich by working hard. This man lived in a small town and the people in the town wanted to be rich, too. But they didn't like to work very hard. One day, the rich man put a large, dirty box in the middle of the road and then hid behind a bush.

First, a farmer came by. The farmer saw the large, dirty box. He did not pick it up or move it out of the way. He left it where it was. Next, a miller came by. He, too, just walked around the box. Soon a milkmaid came by. She, too, just walked around the box. Many more people came by. They all walked around the box. At the end of the day, a young boy came by. He had been taking care of sheep all day. When he saw the large, dirty box, he picked it up and moved it out of the way. He didn't want anyone to trip on it. Just as the boy was walking away, he noticed something on the ground. It was where the large, dirty box had been. The something on the ground was a bag of gold.

1. What can you say about the people in the story who walked around the box?

   _____

2. Why did the rich man hide behind the bush?

   _____

3. What can you say about the boy in the story?

   _____

4. Where was the gold placed?

   _____

5. Who left the gold?

   _____

6. Why was the gold left?

   _____

© Fearon Teacher Aids FE7965
Reproducible

Skill 3:
Cause and Effect

Explanation

Children need to understand why things happen to get the most from what they are reading. A *cause* makes something happen. It is why something takes place. An *effect* is the result of the cause. It is what happens. Writers often state the cause and then provide the result(s) or effect(s). Other times writers state the effect(s) and then give the cause(s).

Teaching Strategies in Action

Explain to the children that when they read, they should ask themselves *what happened* and *why*. These two questions are probably the most effective ways of figuring out cause and effect relationships.

Teachers can also tell students to be on the lookout for the word *because*, which is often a signal that tells us why something happened. It signals a cause or causes.

Examples:

When the clown did funny tricks, Chris and Helen laughed.
    (cause)   (effect)

Kristin and Douglas wore warm clothing because it was cold outside.
    (effect)   (signal)   (cause)

There are a number of words, such as *so* and *as a result of* that are usually clues to a cause/effect or effect/cause relationship. You can decide whether you want to introduce these words as signal words. These can be confusing for primary-grade students because the words *so* and *as a result of* can either signal a cause or an effect based on how they are used in a sentence. Tell children that the best way to figure out what is a cause or an effect is to ask the *why* and *what happened* questions.

Examples:

Joe was afraid of the noise, so he ran home.
    (cause)   (effect)

Celia let Nora play with her toys, so Nora would be happy.
    (effect)   (cause)

Sample Practices

Here are some sample practices that you can use with your students:

1. Jerod came inside when it started to rain.

Question:
What is the cause and effect in this sentence?
Answer:
Jerod came inside when it started to rain.
    (effect)   (cause)

2. Rita threw her books on the floor because she was angry.

Question:
What is the cause and effect in this sentence?
Answer:
Rita threw her books on the floor because she was angry.
    (effect)   (signal)   (cause)

Modeling Strategy

Mrs. Perry says to her students, "When I read I always ask myself why something happened or why something took place. Then I ask myself what caused it to happen. When I ask myself these questions, they help me understand what I am reading."

"These questions also help me when I am writing a story. When we write a story, we want it to make sense. When something happens, we have to have a reason or reasons for its happening. What happens in the story should have a cause or causes."

Mrs. Perry then says, "Let's look at some sentences together."
Here they are:
1. Because Jill didn't feel well, she stayed inside. (cause - effect)
2. Nadine laughs a lot when she sees something funny. (effect - cause)
3. When Lee fell, he hurt his leg. (cause - effect)

"First I ask myself, 'Why did Jill stay inside?' The reason is because she didn't feel well. The word *because* signals a cause. However, I already know it's a cause because the words 'she didn't feel well' answer the question 'Why?' I then ask myself, 'What happened?' that should give me the effect or the result. The effect or result is that Jill stayed inside." Mrs. Perry then asks her students to do the same for the other two sentences.

When working with young children, it is a good idea to introduce cause and effect relationships by using concrete examples. Here is how one first grade teacher, Mrs. Hill, does this. The children are sitting in their seats. Mrs. Hill has previously placed a bag with something in it in the middle of the floor. Mrs. Hill purposely trips over the bag. She stops, looks at the children, and says, "Did you see what just happened?" The children say

"Yes, you tripped." "You're correct," says Mrs. Hill. "I tripped. Why did I trip?" The children reply, "Because there was a bag on the floor. You didn't see the bag." "Good," says Mrs. Hill. "Today we will be working with cause and effect. The cause tells us why something happened and the effect tells us what happened. Now, listen to this sentence: 'Mrs. Hill tripped because there was a bag on the floor.' Let's see if someone can tell me what happened or the effect." "Good, Sharon, 'Mrs. Hill tripped' is correct. Now, who can tell me the cause or why it happened?" "Good, Seth, yes, the answer is 'because there was a bag on the floor.'"

"Did you notice that the word *because* helps us figure out the cause, which is why something happens?" Mrs. Hill then asks her students to act out some cause and effect relationships that she gives them.

Mrs. Hill asks who would like to act out falling down and crying. After a child play-acts falling down and crying, Mrs. Hill asks the children to tell what happened and why it happened—or the cause. Next, she asks the children to construct a sentence telling what happened. Here are some of the sentences the children made up:

Amy cried when she fell.
Because Amy fell, she cried.
Amy cried because she fell.

Mrs. Hill goes over the sentences with the children and has the children tell what happened and why. She asks the children to notice how the word *because* helped them figure out the cause or why something happened. Also, even though the sentences are written differently, the cause and effect are the same. (Amy fell - cause); (Amy cried - effect)

Learning Objective

To figure out cause and effect relationships within the story.

Directions for Student Practices

Use the student practices on pages 51–55 to help your students acquire, reinforce, and review cause and effect. Pick and choose the practices based on the needs and developmental levels of your students. Answers for the student practice pages are on page 170.

When practicing finding cause and effect within a story, have the children read the story and then answer the questions. For those who have difficulty reading, read the story aloud to the children and orally ask them the questions.

Extensions

Role Playing
Invite children to choose a cause/effect scene from a favorite story or make up their own scene with a cause/effect. Divide the class into small groups and encourage each group to act out their cause/effect scene for the class. Challenge the children watching the scenes to discover what is the cause and then what is the effect in each scene.

Cartoons
Invite children to choose a cause/effect situation from a favorite story or make up their own situation with a cause and effect. Then encourage children to draw cartoons of the situations. Ask each child to share his or her cause/effect cartoon with the class.

Write or Tell a Story
Ask students to write sentences on strips of paper that have a cause and effect. Place the paper strips in a large can. Once you have a variety of cause/effect sentences in the can, invite students to pull out a sentence (not their own) and use the sentences to write or tell their own stories.

Skill 3: Cause and Effect

Student's Name _____

Assessment Tool Progress Report

Progress

Improvement

Comments

© Fearon Teacher Aids FE7965
Reproducible

Skill 3: Cause and Effect

Name _____

Practice 1

Directions: Read the make-believe story about Zip and Zap, an imaginary cat and rat who live on the moon. Read the sentences that follow the story. Label which part of the sentence is a cause and which is an effect. (Remember, why something happens is the **cause** and what happens is the **effect**.)

Today is a special day on the moon because it is Children's Day. Zip and Zap love this day because there are lots of parties. The parties are fun because the children play lots of games. Funny clowns do lots of tricks that make the children laugh. The children eat all the things they like and have fun all day long.

1. Today is a special day on the moon because it is Children's Day.

_____

2. Zip and Zap love this day because there are lots of parties.

_____

3. The parties are fun because the children play lots of games.

_____

4. Funny clowns do lots of tricks that make the children laugh.

_____

© Fearon Teacher Aids FE7965
Reproducible

Skill 3: Cause and Effect

Name _____

Practice 2

Directions: Read the make-believe story about Zip and Zap, an imaginary cat and rat who live on the moon. Read the sentences that follow the story. Label which part of the sentence is a cause and which is an effect. (Remember, why something happens is the **cause** and what happens is the **effect**.)

Zip and Zap ate too much, so they got stomachaches. The next day, they both had to stay home because they did not feel well. They did not want to eat anything. They did not want to look at food because it made them sick. Zip and Zap went to see the doctor because their stomachs hurt so much. The doctor gave them medicine to make them feel better. Zip and Zap said that they would not eat so much ever again.

1. Zip and Zap ate too much, so they got stomachaches.

   _____

2. The next day, they both had to stay home because they did not feel well.

   _____

3. They did not want to look at food because it made them sick.

   _____

4. Zip and Zap went to see the doctor because their stomachs hurt so much.

   _____

© Fearon Teacher Aids FE7965
Reproducible

Skill 3: Cause and Effect

Name _____

Practice 3

Directions: Read the short story. Read the sentences that follow the story. Label which part of the sentence is a cause and which is an effect. (Remember, why something happens is the **cause** and what happens is the **effect**.)

Naomi and Phil didn't play outside for two days because their dads said it was too cold. Naomi and Phil, however, wanted to go outside and play. Naomi wanted to go see Phil. "No," said Naomi's dad. "It's too cold outside." "But, I don't have anything to do," said Naomi. "Phil has lots of games, so I want to visit him." It was no fun when it was too cold to play outside.

1. Naomi and Phil didn't play outside for two days because their dads said it was too cold.

   _____

2. Phil has lots of games, so I want to visit him.

   _____

3. It was no fun when it was too cold to play outside.

   _____

© Fearon Teacher Aids FE7965
Reproducible

Skill 3: Cause and Effect

Name _____

Practice 4

Directions: Read the short story. Read the sentences that follow the story. Label which part of the sentence is a cause and which is an effect. (Remember, why something happens is the **cause** and what happens is the **effect**.)

Karesha was bored because she didn't have anything to do. She tried to think of something to do. She thought and thought and thought. Then she asked her mother what she could do because she couldn't think of anything. "Why don't you read a book?" said Karesha's mother. "Your brother knows you love to read, so he brought you lots of new books from the library. Let's look at a few of the books together. I like this one because it is so funny," said her mother.

1. Karesha was bored because she didn't have anything to do.

   _____

2. Then she asked her mother what she could do because she couldn't think of anything.

   _____

3. Your brother knows you love to read, so he brought you lots of new books from the library.

   _____

4. I like this one because it is so funny.

   _____

Name _____

Practice 5

Directions: Read the short story. Read the sentences that follow the story. Label which part of the sentence is a cause and which is an effect. (Remember, why something happens is the **cause** and what happens is the **effect**.)

Burt went on vacation with his family to Mexico. Linda went with her family to Seattle because she wanted to visit her cousins. After their vacations, both Burt and Linda went back to school. Burt was very happy to see Linda. Linda was also happy to see Burt. "I like school because there are lots of things to do," said Burt. "Because I like to learn about things, I like school, too," said Linda. The children were all happy when Burt and Linda came back to school. Burt and Linda are a lot of fun, so the other children missed them.

1. Linda went with her family to Seattle because she wanted to visit her cousins.

   _____

2. "I like school because there are lots of things to do."

   _____

3. "Because I like to learn about things, I like school, too."

   _____

4. The children were all happy when Burt and Linda came back to school.

   _____

5. Burt and Linda are a lot of fun, so the other children missed them.

   _____

Skill 4: Finding the Main Idea of a Paragraph

Explanation

The main idea of a paragraph is what the paragraph is about. Without a main idea, a paragraph would just be a confusion of sentences. All the sentences in a paragraph should help to develop the main idea.

Finding the main idea of a paragraph is a very important skill. It is also one in which children need a great amount of practice. It is not easy to find the main idea of a paragraph. Even if the main idea is directly stated, children still need to be able to figure out that it is, indeed, the main idea—there is no red flag identifying it.

Another problem with finding the main idea is that often children are asked to find the main idea of a paragraph that is not cohesive. In other words, the paragraph is not well written and may actually have more than one main idea. A paragraph must have only one main idea.

Special Note

Even though the procedures for finding the main idea of a paragraph and the central idea of a *group* of paragraphs are similar, finding the main idea and central idea are being presented separately. This helps to highlight the differences between finding the main idea of a paragraph and finding the central idea of a group of paragraphs. (see page 67, Skill 5)

Teaching Strategies in Action

To find the main idea of a paragraph, students must determine what common element the sentences in the paragraph share. Although there is no foolproof method for finding the main idea, there is a widely used procedure that has proven to be very helpful.

Explain to your students that a paragraph is always written about someone or something. The someone or something is the topic of the paragraph. The writer is interested in telling his or her readers something about the topic of the paragraph. To find the main idea, your students must determine what the topic of the paragraph is and what the author is trying to say about the topic that is special or unique. Once students have found these two things, they should have the main idea.

Example:

> Bonnie looked out the window and saw that it was a beautiful, sunny day. Bonnie put on her jacket and went outside. She decided to walk around the block and see what she could see. On her walk, she saw a bluebird, a squirrel, and a bright yellow flower. Bonnie was happy that she went on her walk.

The who or what of the paragraph is "Bonnie." The special or unique thing about Bonnie is that she took a walk and saw many things as she walked around the block. Therefore, the main idea of the paragraph is, "Bonnie saw many things on her walk."

Sample Practices

Here are some sample practices that you can use with your students.

1. Have your students read the following one-paragraph story. Then ask students to choose the sentence that best states the main idea of the paragraph.

    Tom and Jim are upset. For the first time, they will not be in the same class. Tom and Jim are best friends. They have been in the same class since kindergarten. They like being together and doing their homework together. They also like being on the same class team. Now things will change.

    a. Tom and Jim are upset.
    b. Tom and Jim are best friends.
    c. Tom and Jim are upset because they will not be in the same class.
    d. Tom and Jim do everything together.
    e. Tom and Jim like doing things together.

Answer:

   c. Tom and Jim are upset because they will not be in the same class. (Help children understand why this is the correct answer. Go over the other answers and explain why they are not correct. The other choices are all too specific—they are just details. Go over the correct answer and show how all the sentences in the paragraph develop the main idea.)

2. Present the following paragraph to your students:

    Sharon was sad. She felt like crying. She still couldn't believe it. Her best friend, Maria, had moved away. Her best friend had left her. What could she do?

Ask your students what the topic of the paragraph is or about whom or what the paragraph is written.

Answer:

Sharon.

Then ask your students what the writer is saying that is special about Sharon.

Answer:

Sharon is sad because her best friend moved away.

Explain to your students that finding the main idea of the paragraph is finding who or what the paragraph is about and what is special about that who or what. Tell them that all the sentences should help develop the main idea. Go over each sentence with the children.

Modeling Strategy

Here is how Ms. Juarez models the technique for finding the main idea for the following paragraph:

Paul Jones wasn't a liar; he just exaggerated a lot. Paul exaggerated so much that people always expected him to exaggerate. Paul never disappointed them. Here are some examples of Paul's exaggerations. If Paul ate three pancakes, he'd say, "I ate 50 pancakes." If he walked a mile, he'd say, "I walked a 100 miles today."

After reading the paragraph, Ms. Juarez says, "First I ask myself what is the topic of the paragraph? Asking the question who or what can help me get the topic, so I'll try that. Here are some of my choices." Ms. Juarez writes the following choices on the board while pointing out how she found these choices.

a. lying
b. Paul's lying.
c. Paul's exaggeration.
d. exaggeration

Ms. Juarez continues, "After looking at my choices, I choose 'c —Paul's exaggeration.' I chose it because it best answers what the paragraph is about, but I know that this is not the main idea; it is only part of it. I have to go on and ask myself some other things. Now, I have to decide what the writer is saying about Paul's exaggeration that is special and helps pull all the details together. Here are my choices." Ms. Juarez writes the following choices on the board:

a. It is bad.
b. It is not a problem.
c. It is a problem.
d. It applies to everything he does.
e. It should not be allowed.

"I choose 'd.— It applies to everything he does.' The topic is Paul's exaggeration, and what is special about it is that it applies to everything he does. Therefore, the main idea is Paul's exaggeration applies to everything he does."

After Ms. Juarez models this example, she uses other appropriate paragraphs to continue the modeling process with her students. She also asks her students to help her make the choices for finding the main idea of the paragraphs, continuing to say aloud the thinking process involved.

Learning Objective

To determine the main idea of a one-paragraph story and also supply a title for the story.

Directions for Student Practices

Use the student practices on pages 62–66 to help your students acquire, reinforce, and review finding the main idea of a paragraph. Pick and choose the practices based on the needs and developmental levels of your students. Answers for the student practice pages are on pages 170–171.

When practicing finding the main idea for a one-paragraph story, have the children read the story and then answer the questions. For those who have difficulty reading, read the story aloud to the children and orally ask them the questions.

Special Note

In the directions section of the main idea practices, students are asked to find the main idea of a short one-paragraph story rather than of a paragraph. Usually a story has more than one paragraph. However, in working with young children, the use of the term *story* seems more appropriate.

Extensions

Idea Art

After reading a favorite story with the class, give each child a piece of paper. Read an appropriate paragraph or paragraphs from the story and invite the children to draw pictures showing the main idea of each paragraph. Encourage children to share their drawings with the rest of the class.

What's in a Name?

Invite students to choose paragraphs from a favorite story. Have the students read the paragraphs carefully or read them aloud together. Then encourage students to create titles for the chosen paragraphs.

Pantomime

Help children choose appropriate paragraphs from a favorite story. Or, have the children write short paragraphs. Divide the class into small groups and invite each group to pantomime the main idea of the chosen paragraph. Use different paragraphs for each group and invite the other children to guess what each group is pantomiming.

Character to Character

If students are reading a story having several characters, invite children to role play each character. Have one of the characters tell another story character what the main idea of that particular paragraph is.

Skill 4: Finding the Main Idea of a Paragraph

Student's Name _____

Assessment Tool Progress Report

Progress

Improvement

Comments

© Fearon Teacher Aids FE7965
Reproducible

Skill 4: Finding the Main Idea of a Paragraph

Name _____

Practice 1

Directions: Read the make-believe story about Zip and Zap, an imaginary cat and rat who live on the moon. Read the sentences that follow the story. Choose the sentence that best states the main idea of the story. Then write a title for the story that tells what the story is about.

Today is Zip and Zap's birthday. They were both born on the same day and every year they celebrate their birthdays together. They always have a party. They invite all the other boy and girl cats and rats. They eat cake and ice cream and have lots of fun. They play fun games and get lots of presents. Zip and Zap love their birthday parties.

1. Zip and Zap's birthday.

2. Zip and Zap like to have fun.

3. Zip and Zap always have a birthday party.

4. Zip and Zap's birthdays are fun.

5. Zip and Zap play games at their birthday party.

Title: _____

_____

Name _____

Skill 4: Finding the Main Idea of a Paragraph

Practice 2

Directions: Read the make-believe story about Zip and Zap, an imaginary cat and rat who live on the moon. Read the sentences that follow the story. Choose the sentence that best states the main idea of the story. Then write a title for the story that tells what the story is about.

Zip and Zap are not feeling very happy. They have just had their first fight. Zip and Zap have never had a fight before. Zip thought about the fight. Zap thought about the fight. They both felt sad.

1. Zip and Zap are sad.

2. Zip and Zap never had a fight before.

3. Zip and Zap's first fight makes them feel sad.

4. Zip and Zap's fight.

5. Zip and Zap fight with each other.

Title: _____

_____

_____

© Fearon Teacher Aids FE7965
Reproducible

Skill 4: Finding the Main Idea of a Paragraph

Name _____

Practice 3

Directions: Read the make-believe story about Zip and Zap, an imaginary cat and rat who live on the moon. Read the sentences that follow the story. Choose the sentence that best states the main idea of the story. Then write a title for the story that tells what the story is about.

Zip and Zap spend a lot of time in their house. They have to because it is very hot when the sun is out. It gets very cold when the sun is not out. On the moon, daylight lasts for 14 Earth days. Darkness or nighttime lasts for 14 Earth days, too.

1. It's cold on the moon.

2. Zip and Zap stay in their house a lot.

3. The moon's weather.

4. Zip and Zap's house.

5. The moon's weather forces Zip and Zap to stay in their house.

Title: _____

_____

_____

Skill 4: Finding the Main Idea of a Paragraph

Name _____

Practice 4

Directions: Read the short story. Write the main idea of the story. Then write a title for the story that tells what the story is about.

One beautiful, sunny day, a new family moved into a house in Beth's neighborhood. Everyone in the neighborhood was excited. For weeks and weeks, everyone had been talking about the new family's move to the neighborhood. The new family moved into a large house right next to Beth's house. The children in the new family, Jack and Melanie, would be able to play with Beth and her friends. They would also go to Beth's school. Soon the new family would be part of the neighborhood.

Main idea: _____

_____

_____

Title: _____

_____

_____

© Fearon Teacher Aids FE7965
Reproducible

Skill 4: Finding the Main Idea of a Paragraph

Name _____

Practice 5

Directions: Read the short story. Write the main idea of the story. Then write a title for the story that tells what the story is about.

Fiona got an invitation to a birthday party. She didn't feel like going to the party. Her mom asked her why she didn't want to go. "Because I won't know very many people there," she answered. Fiona's mom said, "The more parties you miss, the more people you won't get to know." Fiona sat and thought about this. She thought about the blond-haired girl who seemed nice. She might be at the party and maybe they could be friends. Fiona thought about the funny boy with the purple tennis shoes. He's probably nice, too, she thought. "Maybe I'll go to the party after all," Fiona said.

Main idea: _____

_____

_____

Title: _____

_____

_____

© Fearon Teacher Aids FE7965
Reproducible

Skill 5:
Finding the Central Idea of a Story

Explanation

We generally use the term *central idea* when we refer to a group of paragraphs or a story. The technique for finding the central idea is similar to finding the main idea. The central idea is the central thought of the story. All the paragraphs of the story should develop the central idea.

In the primary grades, the term *main idea* is used more often than central idea. In this book, the two are being presented separately to show that there are differences between the two.

Teaching Strategies in Action

To find the central idea of a story, students must find the common element the paragraphs in the story share. Usually the first paragraph is very helpful because it often contains or anticipates the central idea.

As already stated, the procedure for finding the central idea is similar to that for finding the main idea. Help your students recognize that a story, like a paragraph, is written about someone or something. The "someone" or "something" is the topic of the story. The writer is interested in telling his or her readers something about the topic of the story. To find the central idea of the story, your students must determine what the topic of the story is and what the author is trying to say about the topic that is special or unique. Once they have found these two things, they should have the central idea.

Example:

Jerry wasn't happy about playing on the baseball team. His mom had signed him up. Even though he didn't really want to play, he thought he had to play anyway.

It was the first day of practice and Jerry was late for the game. He forgot his baseball shoes, too. He even couldn't remember which field they were playing on. As Jerry was getting to the ball park, his mom pulled up in the car.

"Jerry, wait!" she cried. "I just found out that your piano lesson has been rescheduled to Thursdays. That's today. I'm so sorry, Jerry. I guess you won't be able to play baseball on Thursdays."

"I guess not," said Jerry, with a secret smile on his face.

In this short story, the topic of the story—the who or what—is Jerry. What is special about Jerry is that he is happy that he doesn't have to be on the baseball team. The central idea then is "Jerry is happy that he doesn't have to be on the baseball team." Students usually can find the central idea in the first paragraph or clues to what it is.

Sample Practices

Here are some sample practices that you can use with your students.

1. Have your students read the following short story. Then have students chose the sentence that best states the central idea of the story.

> Jesse wanted some very special seeds. She wanted purple petunia seeds. Jesse wanted to plant the seeds in her garden.
>
> Jesse looked in three different stores to find the seeds. Finally, she found some purple petunia seeds at the fourth store. She took the seeds home and planted them in her garden. That spring, Jesse had beautiful purple petunias covering her garden.

a. Purple petunia seeds.
b. Jesse wanted purple petunia seeds to plant in her garden.
c. Jesse went to four different stores that day.
d. Purple petunias covered Jesse's garden.

Answer:

> b. Jesse wanted purple petunia seeds to plant in her garden. (Help children understand why this is the correct answer. Go over the other answers and explain why they are not correct. The other choices are all too specific—they are just details. Go over the correct answer and show how this central idea is found in the first paragraph.)

2. Present the following story to your students:

> Tonya had 14 teddy bears. She took very good care of the bears. Tonya always knew where they were. She would dress the bears and play with them and sit them all around the table for tea. Tonya would not let anyone else play with her bears. She wouldn't even let her little sister, Sarah, play with them—unless, of course, Sarah was invited to tea, too.
>
> One day, Tonya came home and found that her favorite bear, Sir Honeypot, was missing from his place on the bed. Tonya looked every where for Sir Honeypot—under the table, in the closet, even in the

kitchen under the sink! Sir Honeypot was nowhere to be found.
As Tonya walked past Sarah's room on her way to look in the bath room, she peered in. There was Sarah, sitting on her bed, having a very involved discussion with Sir Honeypot. Tonya was angry at first. But then she decided that she would let Sarah and Sir Honeypot finish their "conversation."

Ask your students what the topic of the story is or about whom or what the story is written.

Answer:

Tonya.

Then ask your students what the writer is saying that is special about Tonya.

Answer:

Tonya looks all over for her favorite bear, Sir Honeypot, and finally finds him with her little sister, Sarah.

Explain to your students that finding the central idea of the story is finding who or what the story is about and what is special about the subject. Tell them that all the paragraphs should develop the central idea.

Modeling Strategy

Here is how Ms. Davis models this technique for the following short story:

Jeff had always wanted to be a basketball player. His goal was to make the school basketball team. His whole life was directed to making his dream come true. All he thought about was basketball. Everything he did was related to basketball. It was the most important thing in his life.

Jeff practiced for hours every day. He exercised, ate well, and slept at least eight hours a day. He only read books that had to do with basketball. He read the life stories of famous basketball players. Jeff could tell you almost anything you wanted to know about well-known basketball players.

After reading the story, Ms. Davis said "I begin by asking myself what is the topic of the story. In other words, who or what is this story about. It seems to me that the story is about Jeff's goal to be on the school basketball team. Both paragraphs talk about Jeff's goal to be on the basketball team. So the topic is, 'Jeff's goal is to be on the basketball team.' "

"Now, I need to figure out what is special about Jeff's goal to be on the basketball team. It seems that for Jeff, being on the team is the most important thing in his life. Therefore, the central idea is, 'Jeff's goal to be on the basketball team is the most important thing in Jeff's life.'"

"I can check my central idea by rereading the first paragraph because, many times, a writer will state the central idea in the first paragraph. I also can check to see if all the paragraphs develop the central idea."

Learning Objective

To state the central idea of a story and supply a title for the story.

Directions for Student Practices

Use the student practices on pages 73–77 to help your students acquire, reinforce, and review finding the central idea of a story. Pick and choose the practices based on the needs and developmental levels of your students. Answers for the student practice pages are on page 171.

When practicing finding the central idea of a story, have the children read the story and then answer the questions. For those who have difficulty reading, read the story aloud to the children and orally ask them the questions.

Extensions

Three-Panel Display

Invite children to make a three-panel cardboard display to illustrate the central idea of a favorite story. Give each child a large piece of cardboard, approximately 2 feet (61 cm) long. Help children fold the boards in two spots, making three 8-inch (20.3 cm) panels. Then invite children to cover each of the panels with different-colored construction paper. Encourage children to use crayons, paint, or markers to decorate their panels. The first panel can show the main character or characters of the story. The second panel can be a picture of the topic—the who or what—of the story. The third panel can show what is special about the topic. Then invite each child to write or dictate the central idea of the story along the top or bottom of the three panels. Display in the classroom.

Story Posters

Invite each child to make a poster advertising a favorite story. Give each child a piece of posterboard or chart paper. Challenge the children to include the central idea of the story in each of their posters, either in drawings or in written words. Encourage the children to be creative.

Radio Advertisement

Have students write and record a pretend radio advertisement for a favorite story. Divide the class into small groups. Encourage the children in each group to work together to create an advertisement. Children should include the central idea of the stories in their ads. After the children have rehearsed their radio ads, invite each group to tape their ad on a tape recorder in another area of the classroom. Play the recordings for the rest of the class.

Write a Letter

Ask each student to write a letter to a friend or family member about a favorite book or story they are reading or have read. Encourage each student to include the central idea in their letter to help explain the story. Students can send the letters, if they wish.

Skill 5: Finding the Central Idea of a Story

Student's Name _____

Assessment Tool Progress Report

Progress

Improvement

Comments

© Fearon Teacher Aids FE7965
Reproducible

Skill 5: Finding the Central Idea of a Story

Name _____

Practice 1

Directions: Read the make-believe story about Zip and Zap, an imaginary cat and rat who live on the moon. Write the central idea of the story. Then write a title for the story that tells readers what the story is about.

One day, Zip said to Zap "Let's do something different." "All right," said Zap, "but what shall we do?" "I don't know," said Zip. "Let's think."

Zip and Zap sat and sat and sat. They thought and thought and thought. Finally, Zap said, "Let's play hide and seek." "Oh, no," said Zip. "We always play that. I want to play something different." "I know," said Zip. "Let's play pin-the-tail-on-the-donkey." "Oh, no," said Zap. "We always play that. Let's play something different." "It's hard to think of something different to do," said Zip. "I'm tired." "So am I," said Zap, "so let's stop."

"You know," Zap said, "we did do something different today." "That's true," said Zip. "We tried to think of something different to do, and it was hard work."

Central idea: _____

_____

_____

Title: _____

_____

_____

© Fearon Teacher Aids FE7965
Reproducible

Skill 5: Finding the Central Idea of a Story

Name _____

Practice 2

Directions: Read the make-believe story about Zip and Zap, an imaginary cat and rat who live on the moon. Write the central idea of the story. Then write a title for the story that tells readers what the story is about.

Zip and Zap were very excited. They were both born on the same day so they had the same birthday. They also had each received a moon bicycle as a birthday present. They couldn't wait to ride them.

After their birthday party, Zip and Zap put on their special moon clothing and their air masks. They went outside to ride their bicycles.

"Whee, look at me go!" said Zip.
"Look at me! Look at me!" said Zap.
"Be careful," said Zip. "If you go over a bump, you will jump up, up, and away."
"I know," said Zap. "I won't hit any bumps."
Zip and Zap rode their bicycles for a long time. They didn't hit any bumps and had a lot of fun.

Central idea: _____

_____

_____

Title: _____

_____

_____

© Fearon Teacher Aids FE7965
Reproducible

Name _____

Practice 3

Directions: Read the short story. Write the central idea of the story. Then write a title for the story that tells what the story is about.

In a faraway country, there lived a very rich man who liked peace and quiet. This man lived in a large house. On one side of the man's house lived a carpenter. On the other side lived another carpenter. Day and night, you could always hear banging coming from both houses. The rich man knew he had to do something.

One day the rich man told both carpenters that he would give them lots of money if they would move. The carpenters were very happy to hear this. Each moved.

They went to the rich man to collect their money. They told him that they had moved. This made the rich man very happy. He gave them the money.

The next day the rich man heard banging from both sides. He rushed to see what it was. When he saw what was causing the banging, he was very angry. The two carpenters had moved. They had moved into one another's houses.

Central idea: _____

_____

_____

Title: _____

_____

_____

Skill 5: Finding the Central Idea of a Story

Name _____

Practice 4

Directions: Read the short story. Write the central idea of the story. Then write a title for the story that tells readers what the story is about.

Once upon a time in Africa, there lived a cruel lion. This lion frightened all the animals in the jungle. No animal was safe from this lion. One day, the animals met and came up with a plan. The plan was not a very good one, but it was the best they could think of. Each day, one animal would go to the lion to be eaten by him. That way, the other animals would know that they were safe for a little while. The lion agreed to the plan, and that is how they lived for a time.

One day, it was the clever fox's turn to be eaten by the lion. Mr. Fox, however, had other plans. Mr. Fox went to the lion's cave an hour late. The lion was very angry. "Why are you so late? I am hungry," he said. Mr. Fox answered, "Oh, I am so sorry to be late, but another very, very big lion tried to catch me. I ran away from him so that you could eat me." When the lion heard about the other lion, he became more angry. "Another lion?" he asked. "I want to see him."

The fox led the lion through the jungle to see the other lion. When they came to a well, the fox stopped. "The other lion is in there," said the fox, motioning toward the well. The lion looked into the well, and he did, indeed, see a lion. He got so angry that he jumped in the well to fight the lion. That was, of course, the end of the lion.

Central idea: _____

_____

_____

Title: _____

_____

_____

© Fearon Teacher Aids FE7965
Reproducible

Skill 5: Finding the Central Idea of a Story

Name _____

Practice 5

Directions: Read the story. Write the central idea of the story. Then write a title for the story that tells readers what the story is about.

There was once a princess who was very sad. She was so sad that she couldn't eat. Every day the princess grew thinner and thinner. "We must do something," said the queen to the king. "Yes, but what can we do?" asked the king. "We must speak to the wise men," said the queen.

The wise men were called to appear before the king and queen. The wise men told the king and queen that they had to find out why the princess was sad. Once the princess stopped being sad, she would eat. "That is wise," said both the king and queen together. With that, the wise men left. The king and queen went to the princess. "Why are you sad?" asked both the king and queen together. "I am sad because I have no one to play with," said the princess. "But everyone is your friend," said the queen. "I don't want grown-up friends. I want someone my own age," answered the princess. "If we find you someone to play with, will you stop being sad?" asked the king. "If you stop being sad, will you start eating again?" asked the queen. The princess answered "Yes" to both questions.

The king and queen called all their helpers. They told their helpers to find someone for the princess to play with. The helpers went into the village. They found a little girl the same age as the princess. They brought the little girl to the princess. The princess liked the little girl. The princess stopped being sad and started to eat. She stopped growing thinner and thinner.

Central idea: _____

_____

_____

Title: _____

_____

_____

© Fearon Teacher Aids FE7965
Reproducible

Skill 6:
Following Directions

Explanation

Following directions is a skill children will use throughout their lives. By helping children learn to follow directions carefully, you will also be helping them do better on tests, answer questions more easily, and become more able to supply information. Here are some things that you can do to help your students learn good techniques in following directions.

1. Give your students practice in following directions.

2. Encourage students to ask questions about any direction that they are not sure of or that seems confusing to them.

3. Help your students to understand how important the skill of following directions is.

4. Help your students to understand that the ability to follow directions requires concentration.

5. Explain to students that they should try to avoid reading things into directions that are not there.

6. Impress upon your students the importance of reading directions very carefully.

Teaching Strategies in Action

Help your students recognize the importance of being able to follow directions. Challenge students to give you examples of when people need to follow directions. For example, people most often follow directions when cooking, baking, taking medicine, driving, traveling, repairing, building, taking examinations, doing assignments, or filling out applications. There are hundreds of common activities that require the ability to follow directions. Help your students realize that scarcely a day goes by without the need to follow directions. After stressing the importance of directions, involve your students in following directions that you give orally.

Examples:

1. Say to the students, "Write the number three on the board and clap your hands twice."

2. You can have the children try following directions with any number of simple directions. After you have done a few of these orally, put the following geometric figures and sentence on the board.

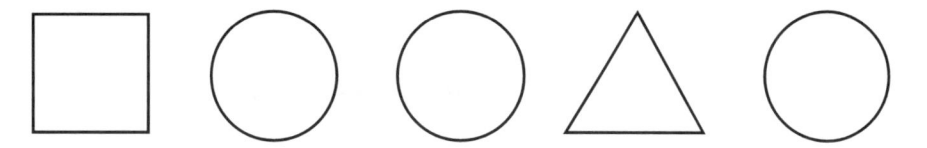

□ ○ ○ △ ○

Put a circle around the second circle. Put an "X" in the first circle.

Read the directions with the children. Then ask for a volunteer to come to the board to carry out the directions. You could try a few of these with the children. To stress concentration, have them read the instructions once only and then carry them out.

Sample Practices

Here are some sample practices that you can use with your students.

1. List the following directions on the chalkboard or read them aloud to the children.

    a. Place your hands on your hips with your feet together.
    b. Put your right foot out, heel to the floor.
    c. Bring your right foot back to original position.
    d. Put your left foot out, heel to the floor.
    e. Bring your left foot back to original position.
    f. Turn once around and clap your hands.

    Encourage the children to follow the directions once more. Explain that if they follow the directions correctly, they will be doing a little jig!

2. Give each student a sheet of paper. Write the following directions on the chalkboard or give the directions orally.

    a. Write the word *hello*.
    b. Change the "e" to an "a."
    c. Change the second "l" to an "a."
    d. Move the "h" so it directly follows the second "a."
    e. Place the second "a" where the "o" is and move the "o" to where the second "a" is.

    Explain to the children that if they followed directions carefully, they should have the word *aloha*, which means *hello* in Hawaiian.

Modeling Strategy

Mrs. Green feels it would help the children if she were to verbalize everything she thinks and does when she is doing a following-directions activity. She presents the children with the following on a sheet of paper:

A E G H 4 7 9 cat book down

Directions: If there is a fifth letter of the alphabet, put a circle around it. If the letter G comes directly after the letter A and before the letter H, put a circle around it. If there is a word the opposite of *up*, put a line under it. If there is a number that equals three less than 12, put a line under it. If there is a word that rhymes with *house* put a circle around the word.

Mrs. Green also puts the same material on the chalkboard. She then says to the children, "I need to read the directions carefully, so I'll do that first. I will make sure that I read every single word. After I read all the directions, I'll do each one carefully. All the directions begin with the word *if*. I better be careful because I may not have to do anything. The first direction says that if there is a fifth letter of the alphabet, put a circle around it. I know my alphabet. The fifth letter is E. There is an E, so I will put a circle around it." Mrs. Green draws a circle around the E on the board and invites the students to do the same on their papers.

Mrs. Green continues. "The second direction is a little more involved. I better be careful. I'll do it in parts. The first part says that if the letter G comes directly after the letter A... wait a moment. On the sheet of paper and on the board, the letter G comes directly after E. The important word is *directly*. G does come after A, but it doesn't come *directly* after A. I don't have to go any further because it is not true. I don't have to do anything."

Mrs. Green stops at this point and asks her students to do the rest of the directions with her. She goes over each direction with the children and shows them on the chalkboard what it should look like. Here is what the finished exercise should look like:

A (E) G H 4 7 <u>9</u> cat book <u>down</u>

Learning Objective

To carry out written or oral directions.

Directions for Student Practices

Use the student practices on pages 83–92 to help your students acquire, reinforce, and review following directions. Pick and choose the practices based on the needs and developmental levels of your students. Answers for the student practice pages are on pages 171–172.

When practicing following directions, have the children read the directions and then answer the questions. For those who have difficulty reading, read the directions aloud to the children and orally ask them the questions.

Special Note

The student practices in this section do not have directions that ask the students to read the instructions once only. However, for older students, you might have them read the directions once only and then complete the practices.

Extensions

Simon Says

Lead the class in a game of "Simon Says." Gradually make the directions more and more complicated as the game goes on. You may also want to invite children to be the leaders of the game.

Let Me Tell You What to Do

Invite children to give directions. When doing the student practices, learning a game, or putting something together, invite one child to read the directions silently to himself or herself and then give directions to the others on what to do. Try to provide opportunities for all the students to read and explain directions.

Board Game

Invite students to make board games based on favorite stories or books. Divide the class into groups of 4 to 6 children. Using file folders as boards, show students how to make simple trails composed of small squares, each about one inch by one inch (2.5 cm by 2.5 cm). Students can make the trails with "start" and "finish" squares. Invite children to make specific directions for a few of the squares, such as "move 1 square back," "take a free turn," etc. Encourage students to decorate the boards with scenes from the books or stories. Have the students write directions for the games and then have each group share their game with the class.

Skill 6: Following Directions

Student's Name _____

Assessment Tool Progress Report

Progress

Improvement

Comments

Skill 6: Following Directions

Name _____

Practice 1

Directions: Read each instruction carefully. Then carry out the instructions on the boxed material.

□ □ □ △ ○ ○ □ ○

Instructions

1. Put the number **3** in the third square. Put the number **5** in the second circle.

2. Put the number **10** in the triangle. Put the number **2** in the first square.

3. Put a circle around the third circle. Put the number **1** in the third circle.

4. Put an "X" in the second square. Put an "X" on the triangle.

© Fearon Teacher Aids FE7965
Reproducible

Skill 6: Following Directions

Name _____

Practice 2

Directions: Read each instruction carefully. Then carry out the instructions on the boxed material.

Instructions

1. Put the number **9** in the third triangle. Put the number **4** in the second circle.

2. Put the letter **R** in the second square. Put a circle around the fourth triangle.

3. Put an "X" on the first, second, and fifth triangles. Put a circle around the first circle.

4. Put the third letter of the alphabet in the first circle. Put the next to the last letter of the alphabet in the third square and the third circle.

Name _____

Practice 3

Directions: Read each instruction carefully. Then carry the instructions out on the boxed material.

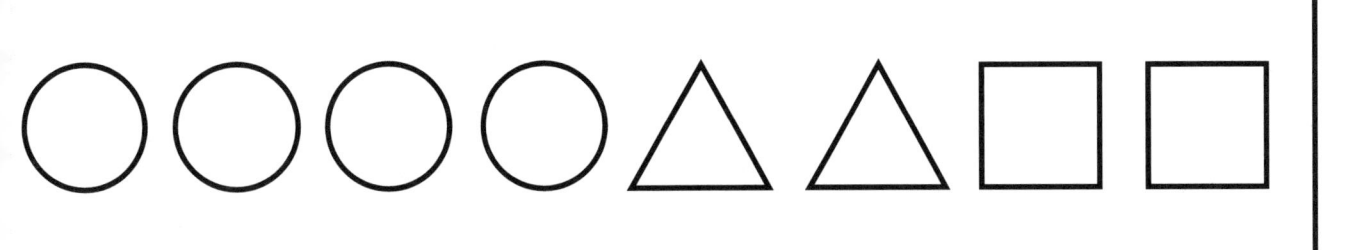

○ ○ ○ ○ ○ △ △ ☐ ☐

Instructions

1. Put the letter **D** in the third circle. Put the number **5** in the first triangle.

2. Put the number that equals 3 + 4 in the first circle. Put the number that equals 4 + 5 in the second square.

3. Put the number that equals 5 + 7 in the second triangle. Put the letter that comes before **F** in the second circle.

4. Put the letter that comes after **R** in the fourth circle. Put the three letters that come before **P** above the first square.

Skill 6: Following Directions

Name _____

Practice 4

Directions: Read each instruction carefully. Then carry out the instructions.

1. Make three circles, two squares, and one triangle. Put a circle around the second circle.

2. Make a square, a triangle, and a circle, one after the other. Put an "X" on each.

3. Make two circles, one triangle, and four squares. Put the letter that comes before **G** in the first circle, the letter that comes after **L** in the triangle, and the letter that comes before **Q** in the first square.

4. Make four circles. Put the next odd number after five in the first circle, the next even number after eight in the last circle, and the letter before **D** in the third circle.

5. Write the odd numbers from one to seven. Write the even numbers from four to ten. Write the four letters of the alphabet that come before **S**.

6. Make six triangles and one square. Put a circle around each of the first four triangles. Put an "X" inside the square.

Skill 6: Following Directions

Name _____

Practice 5

Directions: Read carefully the entire list of directions that follow before doing anything. You have three minutes to finish this activity.

1. Add 5 and 5.

2. Add 17 and 14.

3. Write the last three letters of the alphabet.

4. Write all the odd numbers from 1 to 10.

5. Write all the even numbers from 1 to 10.

6. Write your name at the top of the paper.

7. Write your address at the bottom of the paper.

8. Write the first five letters of the alphabet.

9. Make three squares.

10. Make three triangles.

11. Make a circle, a square, and a triangle.

12. Raise your right hand.

13. Lower your right hand.

14. Turn your paper upside down.

15. Call out, "I am nearly finished."

16. Call out, "I am the best direction follower."

17. Now that you have finished reading everything, do only numbers 6 and 7.

© Fearon Teacher Aids FE7965
Reproducible

Skill 6: Following Directions

Name _____

Practice 6

Directions: Read each instruction carefully. Then carry out the instructions on the boxed material.

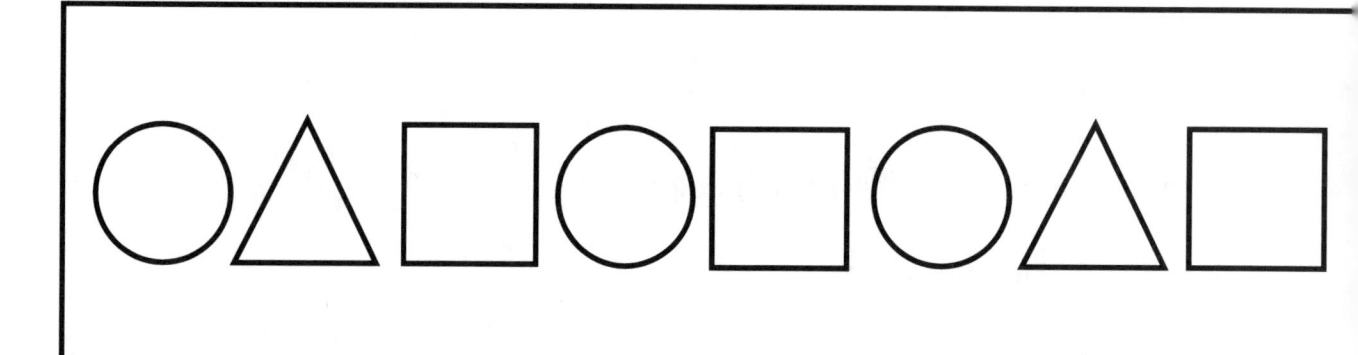

○ △ △ □ ○ □ □ ○ △ □

Instructions

1. If there are three circles and three triangles, put the first letter of the alphabet in the second triangle.

2. If there are the same number of squares as circles, put the letter that comes before **P** in the third circle.

3. If there are more circles than triangles, put the sum of 6 + 5 in the first square.

4. If there are three different figures one after the other, put a circle around all the circles.

Name _____

Practice 7

Directions: Read each instruction carefully. Then carry out the instructions on the boxed material.

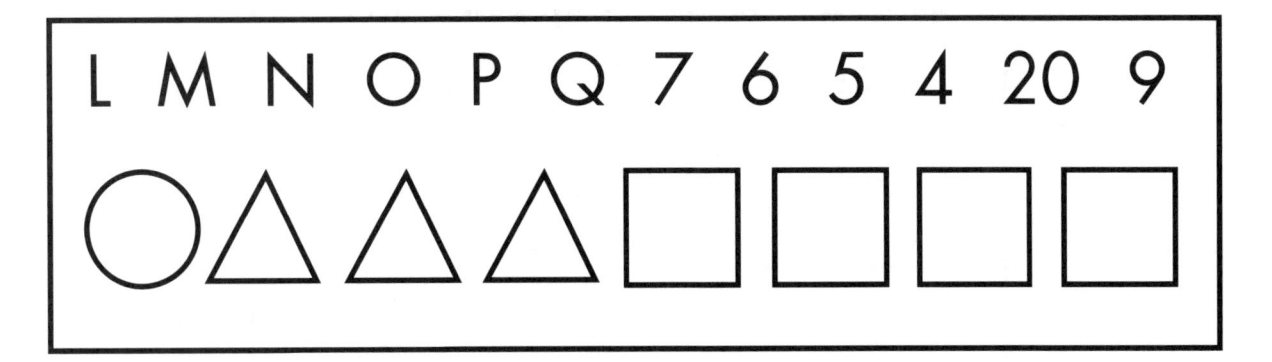

```
L M N O P Q 7 6 5 4 20 9
○ △ △ △ □ □ □ □
```

Instructions

1. If there are more letters than numbers, put an "X" in the first square.

2. If there are two numbers that added together equal another number in the boxed material, put a circle around the second triangle.

3. If there are more squares than triangles and the same number of letters as numbers, put the first letter in the boxed material in the first square after the third triangle.

4. If there are the same number of odd numbers as even numbers and if two numbers added together equal **11**, put the number that comes before **6** in the boxed material in the third square.

Skill 6: Following Directions

© Fearon Teacher Aids FE7965
Reproducible

Skill 6: Following Directions

Name _____

Practice 8

Directions: Read each instruction carefully. Then carry out the instructions on the boxed material.

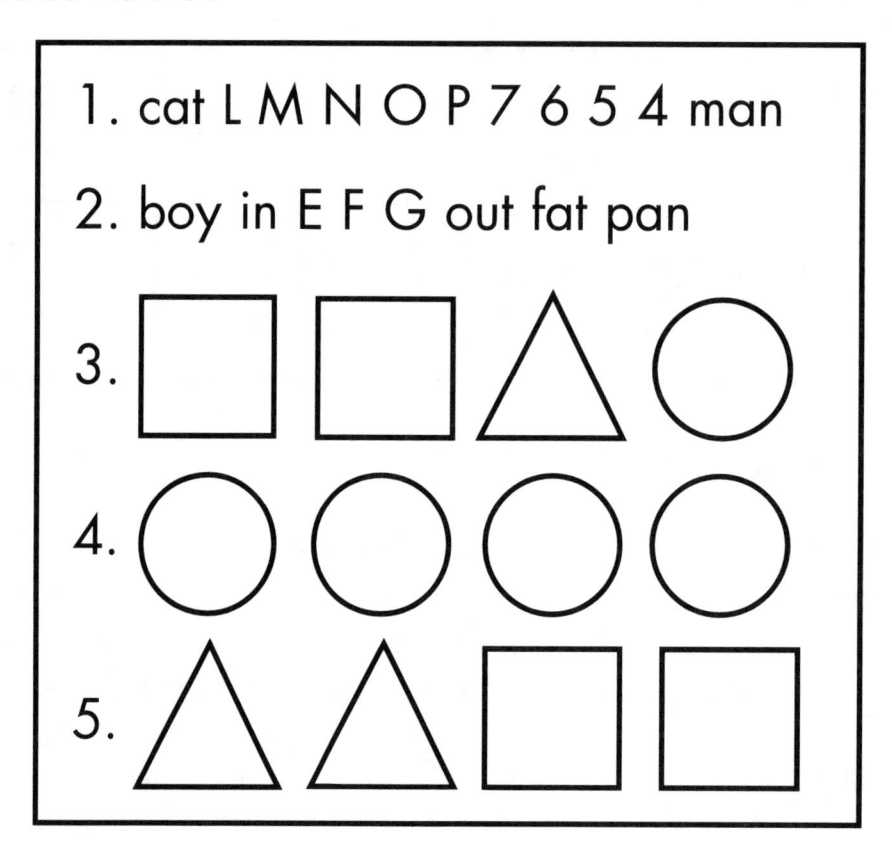

---

1. cat L M N O P 7 6 5 4 man

2. boy in E F G out fat pan

3. ▢ ▢ △ ◯

4. ◯ ◯ ◯ ◯

5. △ △ ▢ ▢

Instructions

1. If there are two words that rhyme with **bat** and one word that rhymes with **pin**, put a circle around the two words that rhyme with **bat**.

2. If there are more circles than squares and if there are more squares than triangles, put an "X" on the word that is the opposite of **girl**.

3. If there are more letters than words and if there are fewer numbers than letters, put a circle around the middle letter in the second row.

4. If there are the same number of squares in row three as in row five and if there are the same number of even numbers as odd numbers, put an "X" above the triangle in the third row.

© Fearon Teacher Aids FE7965
Reproducible

Name _____

Practice 9

Directions: Read each instruction once only. Then carry out each instruction on the circle.

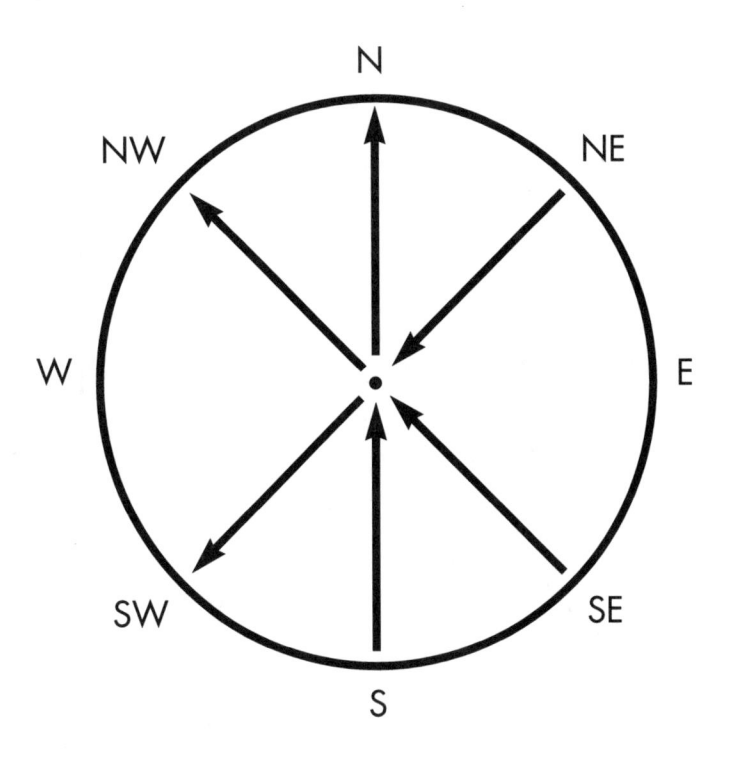

Instructions

1. If the arrows point in all the directions in the circle, put a circle around **NE**.

2. If the arrows point to **N**, **S**, and **NW**, put a circle around **S**.

3. If the arrows point to **N**, **SW**, and **NW**, put an "X" on **N**.

4. If there are more arrows pointing **NW** than **NE**, and if there are two arrows pointing **SW**, put a circle around **E**.

Skill 6: Following Directions

Name _____

Practice 10

Directions: Read each instruction once only. Then carry out each instruction on the circles.

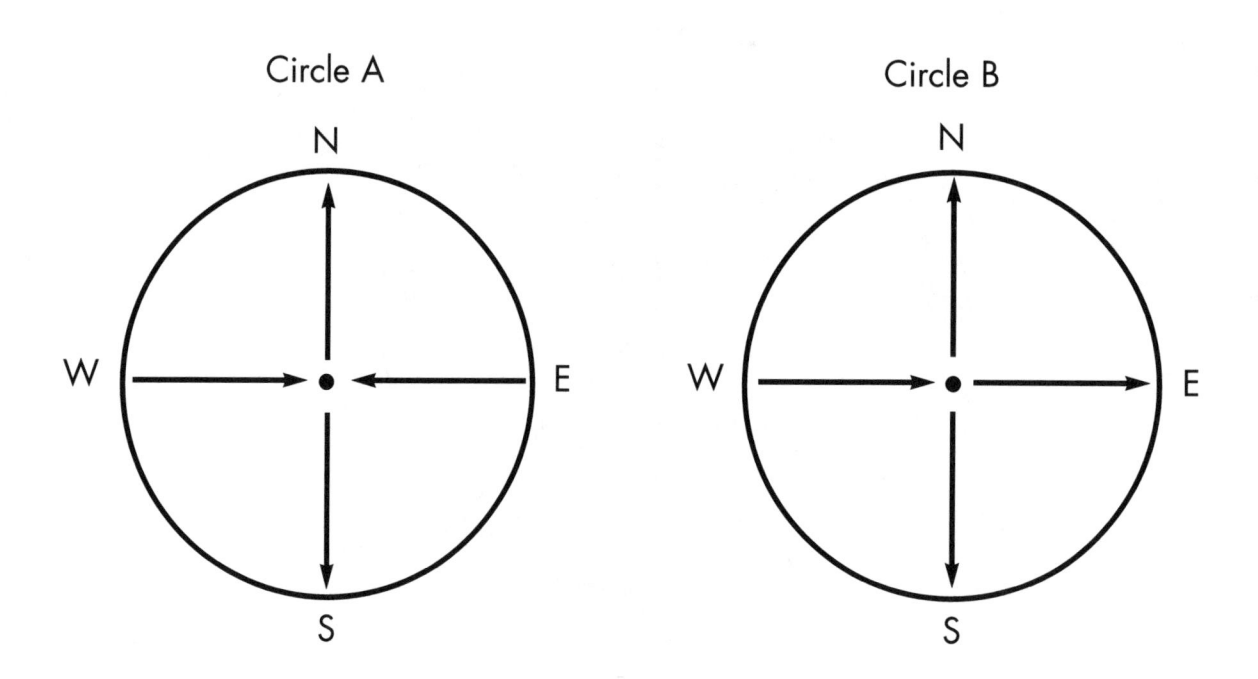

Circle A

Circle B

Instructions

1. If the arrows in Circle A are pointing in the same directions as the arrows in Circle B, put a circle around **E** in Circle A.

2. If the arrows in Circle A are pointing in four different directions, and if the arrows in Circle B are pointing in four different directions, put a circle around **W** in Circle B.

3. If arrows in Circle B are pointing toward **E** and **N**, and arrows in Circle A are pointing toward **E** and **N**, put a circle around **S** in Circle A.

4. If arrows in Circle A are pointing toward **E** and **W**, and arrows in Circle B are pointing toward **E** and **W**, put a circle around **N** in Circle B.

© Fearon Teacher Aids FE7965
Reproducible

Skill 7:
Categorizing

Explanation

The ability to divide items into categories is a very important thinking skill. As children advance through the grades, they should be able to differentiate and group items into more complex categories. Primary-grade children should be able to categorize a cat as distinct from a mouse or a rabbit. They should also be able to group the words *cat, dog,* and *cow* together as animals. As children develop their thinking skills, they should be able to proceed from more generalized classifications to more specialized classifications.

Teaching Strategies in Action

Help your students recognize that every time they put things into groups, such as pets, farm animals, wild animals, cities, states, countries, capitals, fruits, vegetables, colors, and so on, they are using the skill of categorizing. When they categorize things, they are classifying things. To be able to classify things, they must know what belongs together and what does not belong together. You can help your students to classify or categorize things into more general or more specific categories.

Example:
zucchini, carrot, peanut, orange, cashew, lettuce, apple

The category of *food* is more general than the categories of *fruits, vegetables,* or *nuts.*

Example:
dog, lion, horse, tiger, elephant, goat, cat, mouse, bird

The category of *animals* is more general than the categories of *pets, wild animals,* or *tame animals.* The category of *pets* is less general than the category of *animals,* but more general than the categories of *dogs* or *cats.*

Sample Practices

Here are some sample practices that you can use with your students.

1. Write the following list of animals on the chalkboard:
   lion, deer, dog, cat, tiger, parakeet, hamster, panther

Then write the headings *pets* and *wild animals* on the chalkboard. Help the children categorize the animals previously listed into these two new categories.

pets	wild animals
dog	lion
cat	tiger
parakeet	deer
hamster	panther

2. List the following words on the chalkboard. Then ask students to put the words into two categories.

car, rowboat, spaceship, motorcycle, yacht, airplane, truck, bus, helicopter

Explain to students that these are all modes of transportation. They can be categorized as follows:

land transportation	water transportation	air transportation
car	rowboat	airplane
truck	yacht	helicopter
motorcycle		spaceship
bus		

Modeling Strategy

Here is how Mr. Mason helps the children learn about categorizing. He presents the children with the following group of words:

pear, celery, milk, apple, cheese, carrot, plum, butter, banana, spinach

Mr. Mason then says: "I want to group these words into categories. First I look at each of them. They are all things we eat. They are all foods. The group *food* is a very big one. I would like to divide the *food* category into smaller groups. Let me look again at the words. I see fruits, vegetables, and dairy products. I think I can divide the words further into these three groups. Under *fruits*, I will write pear, apple, plum, and banana. Under *vegetables*, I will write celery, carrot, and spinach. Under *dairy products*, I will write milk, cheese, and butter." Mr. Mason then writes the following words on the chalkboard:

vegetables	dairy products	fruits
celery	milk	pear
carrot	cheese	apple
spinach	butter	plum
		banana

© Fearon Teacher Aids FE7965

Mr. Mason then asks the students to give examples of other foods that would fit into each group. As the children state each food and its category, Mr. Mason writes it on the chalkboard under the correct heading.

Learning Objective

To classify items into categories in general and specific classifications.

Directions for Student Practices

Use the student practices on pages 98–117 to help your students acquire, reinforce, and review categorizing. Pick and choose the practices based on the needs and developmental levels of your students. Answers for the student practice pages are on pages 172–174.

When practicing categorizing, have the children read the directions and then answer the questions. For those who have difficulty reading, read the directions aloud to the children and orally ask them the questions.

Special Note

The student practices that are presented for your students are based on graduated levels of difficulty. The first few practices deal with pictorial representations of various items that should be familiar to your students.

Extensions

Categorizing Rocks

Provide the children with a box of assorted rocks. Invite children to think up ways they can categorize the rocks, such as by color, size, shine, shape, or texture.

Character Traits

Divide the class into groups. Invite the children in each group to choose characters from a number of favorite books or stories. Help children write the names of the characters on small strips of paper. Then challenge the children to arrange the character names in groups based on their common traits, such as clever, funny, silly, and so on.

Similar Settings

Write three or four story settings on cardboard signs and place the signs around the classroom. Then invite students to take books from the class library they have read and categorize the books according to their settings.

Genre

Encourage students to choose a favorite story or book they are currently reading and tell what category the book belongs in—adventure, mystery, fiction, humor, nonfiction, fantasy, science fiction, and so on. Then invite students to form groups according to what category their book is in and share their books orally with one another.

Skill 7: Categorizing

Student's Name _____

Assessment Tool Progress Report

Progress

Improvement

Comments

Skill 7: Categorizing

Name _____

Practice 1

Directions: Cut out the pictures and paste the pictures according to their groups—**vegetables, fruits,** or **drinks**—on a blank sheet of paper.

milk

corn on cob

pear

apple

carrot

soda pop

cherries

potato

tomato

water

beet

banana

lemon

© Fearon Teacher Aids FE7965
Reproducible

Skill 7: Categorizing

Name _____

Practice 2

Directions: Cut out the pictures and paste the pictures according to their groups—**pets, farm animals,** or **wild animals**—on a blank sheet of paper.

cat

elephant

dog

hippopotamus

parrot

cow

chicken

horse

lion

giraffe

ape

tiger

Skill 7: Categorizing

Name _____

Practice 3

Directions: Group the various items below under these headings on a blank sheet of paper: **furniture, things used for eating**, and **appliances.**

iron

cup

bed

knife

dresser

oven

plate

fork

spoon

toaster

refrigerator

sofa

© Fearon Teacher Aids FE7965
Reproducible

Skill 7: Categorizing

Name _____

Practice 4

Directions: Group the shapes in as many ways as you can on a blank sheet of paper. You can draw the shapes to make the various groups.

© Fearon Teacher Aids FE7965
Reproducible

Skill 7: Categorizing

Name _____

Practice 5

Directions: Group the cards in as many ways as you can on a blank sheet of paper.

Skill 7: Categorizing

Name _____

Practice 6

Directions: First read the list of words. Then group the words in at least seven different ways.

hen	kitten	ape
drake	goose	tiger
sow	pig	goat
mare	dog	mule
colt	turkey	horse
gander	duck	puppy
elephant		

Skill 7: Categorizing

Name _____

Practice 7

Directions: First read the list of words. Then group the words in at least seven different ways.

chalk	chalkboard	library	jump rope
checkers	science books	desk	auditorium
basketball	pencil	classroom	pen
paper	history books	baseball	chess
principal	monopoly	nurse	spelling books
student	teacher		

© Fearon Teacher Aids FE7965
Reproducible

Name _____

Practice 8

Directions: First read the list of words. Then group the words in at least seven different ways.

scarf	watch	shoes	sweater	pants
socks	bracelet	coat	earrings	slip
cap	stockings	gloves	blouse	tights
shirt	vest	slippers	hat	mittens
dress	jeans	gown	skirt	boots

Skill 7: Categorizing

Name _____

Practice 9

Directions: Read the words in the word list. Choose a word from the word list that would belong in one of the groups listed below. All words from the word list are used as answers. The first is done for you.

Word List: coat, green, circle, milk, Terry, checkers, cat, ten

1. foods   _____milk_____

2. colors   _____

3. clothing   _____

4. animals   _____

5. shapes   _____

6. numbers   _____

7. games   _____

8. names   _____

© Fearon Teacher Aids FE7965
Reproducible

Skill 7: Categorizing

Name _____

Practice 10

Directions: Read the words in the word list. Choose a word from the word list that would belong in one of the groups listed below. All words from the word list are **not** used as answers. The first is done for you.

Word List: peas, carrots, yellow, white, purse, ring, gloves, plums, peaches, raisins, spinach, bread, checkers, football, candy, brown, gown, bathing suit

1. dried fruits   _____raisins_____

2. dark colors   _____

3. outdoor games   _____

4. indoor games   _____

5. cold weather clothing   _____

6. hot weather clothing   _____

7. leafy vegetables   _____

8. jewelry   _____

© Fearon Teacher Aids FE7965
Reproducible

Skill 7: Categorizing

Name _____

Practice 11

Directions: Read the word list. Then choose a word from the word list that would belong to each group of words listed below and add it to the group. All words from the word list are used as answers.

Word List: crayon, wood, ant, goose, Frank, purple, Susan, spinach, circle, door

1. George, Max, Steve _____

2. carrot, beet, bean _____

3. blue, red, orange _____

4. chimney, window, roof _____

5. chalk, pen, pencil _____

6. coal, oil _____

7. wasp, fly _____

8. Mary, Tara, Kathy _____

9. triangle, oval, square _____

10. duck, chicken, turkey _____

Skill 7: Categorizing

Name _____

Practice 12

Directions: Read the word list. Then choose a word from the word list that would belong to each group of words listed below and add it to the group. All words from the word list are **not** used as answers.

Word List: doe, mustard, clothing, pants, eggs, chalkboard, lettuce, raisin, banana, dishwasher, food, six, twenty, candy, eight, seven, lady, princess, sixteen, nineteen, bread

1. apple, pear, plum   _____

2. five, ten, fifteen   _____

3. one, three, five   _____

4. ten, twelve, fourteen   _____

5. king, prince, queen   _____

6. hen, ewe, mare   _____

7. oven, stove, refrigerator _____

8. two, four, six   _____

9. ketchup, relish, mayonnaise _____

10. desk, teacher, student _____

Skill 7: Categorizing

Name _____

Practice 13

Directions: Read the word list. Then choose a word from the word list that would belong to each group of words listed below and add it to the group. All words from the word list are **not** used as answers. A word may be used only once.

Word List: pleasant, tired, thin, wide, large, pretty, leaf, cruel, school, reading, cat, subject, pet

1. big, great _____

2. good-looking, handsome _____

3. nice, friendly _____

4. mean, nasty _____

5. bark, branch _____

6. spelling, math _____

7. hamster, dog _____

Name _____

Practice 14

Directions: Read each group of words. Try to figure out how they belong together. Then read the word list. Choose a word from the word list that best describes each group. All words from the word list are used as answers. The first one is done for you.

Word List: names, nuts, flowers, fowl, fruits, vegetables, meat, clothing, colors, shapes

1. celery, lettuce, peas, beans   _____vegetables_____

2. triangle, circle, square   _____

3. duck, chicken, turkey, goose   _____

4. almond, pecan, acorn   _____

5. mittens, hat, dress, coat   _____

6. gold, purple, red, blue   _____

7. Elena, Theo, Sally, Jack   _____

8. banana, apple, grape   _____

9. rose, mums, tulip   _____

10. pork, lamb, beef   _____

Skill 7: Categorizing

Name _____

Practice 15

Directions: Read each group of words. Try to figure out how they belong together. Then read the word list. Choose a word or phrase from the word list that best describes each group. All words from the word list are **not** used as answers.

Word List: clothing, boys' names, girls' names, names, house things, kitchen things, eating things, bedroom things, food, sweets, tools, school things, writing things, fruit, dried fruit

1. Tasha, Maria, Jane _____

2. George, Paulo, Jerome _____

3. bed, pillow, blanket _____

4. spoon, fork, knife _____

5. prunes, raisins _____

6. crayon, pencil, magic marker _____

7. hammer, saw, pliers _____

8. cookies, candy, cake, apple, bread _____

Skill 7: Categorizing

Name _____

Practice 16

Directions: First read the words in each group. Three of the words in each group belong together and one does not. Circle the word in each group that does **not** belong. The first is done for you.

1. winter, summer, (night), fall

2. December, July, January, February

3. carrot, pea, bean, lime

4. fairy tales, history books, science books, biographies

5. train, truck, car, airplane

6. motorcycle, bicycle, car, scooter

7. fifteen, twenty, twenty-five, twenty-eight

8. California, Ohio, United States, Florida

9. sow, doe, ewe, bull

10. whale, shark, salmon, tuna

© Fearon Teacher Aids FE7965
Reproducible

Skill 7: Categorizing

Name _____

Practice 17

Directions: First read the words in each group. Three of the words in each group belong together and one does not. Circle the word in each group that does **not** belong. The first is done for you.

1. one, nine, (blue,) three

2. duck, goose, chicken, pig

3. basketball, baseball, ice hockey, football

4. violin, harp, cello, piano

5. two, five, three, one

6. eyes, hair, mouth, nose

7. gander, hen, rooster, drake

8. Europe, England, Spain, Mexico

9. raisin, plum, pear, apple

10. fin, hoof, gill, scale

Name _____

Practice 18

Directions: First read the words in each group. Three of the words in each group belong together and one does not. Circle the word in each group that does **not** belong. The first is done for you.

1. kitten, puppy, cub, (duck)

2. China, Asia, North America, Africa

3. east, west, north, right

4. dog, cat, ape, horse

5. drake, mare, rooster, ram

6. milk, cheese, meat, butter

7. student, pupil, learner, teacher

8. cupboard, bag, pantry, closet

9. ham, pork, bacon, beef

10. vest, coat, cape, hat

Skill 7: Categorizing

Name _____

Practice 19

Directions: First read the words in each group. Three of the words in each group belong together and one does not. Circle the word in each group that does **not** belong. The first is done for you.

1. purple, red, (seven), green

2. doe, duckling, puppy, kitten

3. mule, lion, tiger, ape

4. rose, carnation, tree, pansy

5. salt, pepper, sugar, cloves

6. sandal, slipper, shoe, sock

7. sty, stable, silo, coop

8. saw, pliers, knife, scissors

9. chair, bed, bunk, cot

10. beagle, fox, collie, terrier

Name _____

Practice 20

Directions: First read the words in each group. Three of the words in each group belong together and one does not. Circle the word in each group that does **not** belong. The first is done for you.

1. China, Germany, (Africa), France

2. crow, canary, eagle, robin

3. large, long, huge, enormous

4. single, individual, silent, alone

5. rooster, mare, gander, drake

6. palace, castle, mansion, cabin

7. chirp, bark, bray, bell

8. pouch, bag, purse, drawer

9. scarf, necklace, ring, watch

10. frogs, snakes, turtles, lizards

Skill 8:
Completing Word Relationships (Analogies)

Explanation

Analogies are the relationships between words and ideas. Certain words have relationships to one another, such as *night* and *day* (opposites) or *fruit* and *banana* (classification). Working with analogies requires high-level thinking skills. Students must have a good stock of vocabulary as well as the ability to see the relationships between the words or ideas.

Teaching Strategies in Action

Some primary-grade level children can begin to be exposed to simple analogies based on word relationships with which they are familiar. In order to be able to make the best use of analogies or to complete an analogy statement or proportion, the children must know the meanings of the words and the relationship of the pair of words.

> *Example:*
> Sad is to happy as good is to _____.

Many primary-grade level children know the meaning of the words *sad* and *happy* and that *sad* is the opposite of *happy*. Therefore, children would usually be able to complete the analogy statement or proportion with the correct word—*sad*.

There are many relationships that words may have to one another, such as similar meanings, opposite meanings, classification, going from particular to general, going from general to particular, degree of intensity, specialized labels, characteristics, cause-effect, effect-cause, function, whole-part, ratio, and many more. Explain to your students that they can gain clues to the word relationships from the pairs making up the analogies—that is, the words themselves express the relationship.

> *Example:*
> *pretty* is to *beautiful*—the relationship is degree of intensity (the state of being stronger, greater, or more than)
> *hot* is to *cold*—the relationship is one of opposites
> *car* is to *vehicle*—the relationship is one of classification

It would probably be a good idea for you to review the word lists of the presented analogy practices to determine whether your students are familiar with the vocabulary. You can encourage students to use dictionaries to look up any unfamiliar words.

© Fearon Teacher Aids FE7965

The analogy practices (pages 125–139) can be done in small groups or with the entire class orally as well as individually. If children work individually on the analogy practices, you may want to go over the answers together so that interaction and discussion can further enhance children's vocabulary development.

Sample Practices

Here are some sample practices that you can use with your students.

1. Black is to white as night is to _____.
   Answer:

   day

   Explain to children that *black* is the opposite of *white*. So children need to find the opposite of *night*, which is *day*.

2. Dog is to puppy as cat is to _____.
   Answer:

   kitten

   A *puppy* is a baby *dog*, so students need to find what a baby *cat* is called, which is a *kitten*.

3. Hand is to mitten as head is to _____.
   Answer:

   hat

   A *hand* wears a *mitten* to stay warm. So students need to find what keeps a *head* warm, which is a *hat*.

Modeling Strategy

Here is how Ms. Gerber helps her students work with verbal analogies. Ms. Gerber writes the following sets of words on the chalkboard:

happy is to sad	bad is to good
big is to little	fat is to thin

She asks the children to read the sets of words to see how they go together. Ms. Gerber says she will do the same. Ms. Gerber then reads aloud the sets. She says, "Let me see, *happy* is the opposite of *sad*. *Bad* is the opposite of *good*. *Big* is the opposite of *little* and *fat* is the opposite of *thin*. The words in the sets are all opposites." She then writes the following on the chalkboard:

Happy is to sad as bad is to good. Big is to little as fat is to thin.

Ms. Gerber asks the children to read the sets of words and tell her what they notice. Ms. Gerber says she will do the same.

She reads aloud the first set and says, "In the first example, the first set has word opposites and the second set has word opposites. In the second example, the first set has word opposites and the second set also has word opposites. What I notice is that the first and second sets have the same kinds of pairs."

Ms. Gerber then presents the children with the following sets and tells them that they go together in some way.

big is to large   small is to little
finish is to end   start is to begin

Ms. Gerber says aloud her thoughts as she figures out that all these sets are words with the same meaning. She then puts on the chalkboard the following sets and asks the children what they can tell her about the sets.

Big is to large as small is to little.
Finish is to end as start is to begin.
Happy is to sad as bad is to good.
Big is to little as fat is to thin.

Ms. Gerber says, "What I notice again is that the first and second sets of each sentence have the same kinds of pairs. Here are some more sets. Let's see if it's true for these also:

Fall is to season as March is to month.
Apple is to fruit as pea is to vegetable.

"Let me see, *fall* is a season. It is an example of a season. *March* is a month. It is an example of a month. Both sets in the pair are examples. *Apple* is an example of a fruit, and *pea* is an example of a vegetable. The first set has an example and the second set has an example. I see again that when two sets are put together, they have the same kinds of pairs." Ms. Gerber presents the children with the following and asks the children to try to figure out the word relationships.

Daughter is to child as aunt is to relative.

Ms. Gerber asks the children if they noticed that the first set has an example (daughter is to child). She mentions that a *daughter* is a kind of *child*. She then states that the second set also has an example (aunt is to relative). She tells the children that an *aunt* is a kind of *relative*. Ms. Gerber then asks her students to tell her what they learned. Many children raise their hands. Ms. Gerber calls on Seth. Seth says, "When two sets are put together, they must have the same kinds of pairs." "Yes, good," says Ms. Gerber. She then gives the children some verbal analogy exercises to do on their own. Ms. Gerber tells the children she will go over these together with them. However, first she will do one for them, so they can see what she does to get the correct answer. Here is the example:

Autumn is to fall as wealthy is to _____. (poor or rich)

Ms. Gerber tells her students that in order to work with word sets, they must know the meanings of the words. If the students do not know the meanings of the words in the sets, they cannot figure out the relationship between the words. "I know," Ms. Gerber says, "that *autumn* is a season and *fall* is a season. I also know that autumn and fall are the same. They have the same meaning. Therefore, the words in my second set must also have the same meaning. Both sets must have the same kinds of pairs. Therefore, the answer must be *rich*. *Rich* is the same as *wealthy*. They share the same meaning." Now Ms. Gerber feels her students are ready to try the exercises on their own. "Of course, I am here to help anyone who needs help," Ms. Gerber says before the students begin.

Special Note

You may want to use the term *word relationships* with the students rather than *analogies*. You might want to introduce the term *analogy* to some of your older students.

In introducing some of the relationships that pairs of words can have to one another, try to use words that are in your students' listening vocabulary—that is, children have heard the words and know their meanings. The list of some possible relationships (page 118) is presented as an aid for you.

You might want to help students recognize that there may be different ways to describe the relationship between a set of words.

Example:
    hammer is to tool

This word *relationship* can be particular to general, classification, or example.

Learning Objective

To understand the relationships or analogies between words or ideas.

Directions for Student Practices

Use the student practices on pages 125-139 to help your students acquire, reinforce, and review completing word relationships or analogies. Pick and choose the practices based on the needs and developmental levels of your students. Answers for the student practice pages are on pages 174-175.

When practicing completing word relationships, or analogies, have the children read the directions and then answer the questions. For those who have difficulty reading, read the directions aloud to the children and orally ask them the questions.

Special Note

The practices that are presented for your students are based on graduated levels of difficulty. The first eight practices deal with pictorial representations of various items that should be familiar to your students. Special teacher instructions are provided for these eight exercises:

Practices 1 and 2

Present the picture sets to the children. Explain to children that the sets of pictures belong together in some way. Each set has a missing picture. Have each child look at the first pair of pictures in the set. Challenge children to figure out how the pictures belong together. Then have each child choose a picture from the large box that would *best* complete the second pair in the set. Encourage each child to draw a line from the picture in the large box to the appropriate empty space. All the pictures from the large box are used as answers. Do the example with the children.

Practices 3 and 4

The instructions for Practices 3 and 4 are the same as the previous practices. However, all the pictures in the large box are *not* used as answers. Do the example with the children.

Practices 5 and 6

Present the word and picture sets to the children. Explain to the children that the sets of words and pictures belong together in some way. Each set has a missing picture. Have each child look at the first word and picture pair of the example. Challenge children to try to figure out how the words and pictures belong together. Then have each child choose a picture from the large box that would *best* complete the second pair in the set. Encourage each child to draw a line from the picture in the large box to the appropriate empty space. For Practice 6, all pictures in the large box are *not* used as answers.

Practices 7 and 8

Present the picture and word sets to the children. Explain to the children that the sets of pictures and words belong together in some way. Each set has a missing word. Have each child look at the first picture and word pair of the example. Challenge children to figure out how they belong together. Then have each child choose a word from the large box that would best complete the second pair in the set. Encourage each child to write the word in the blank. For Practice 8, all words are *not* used as answers.

Extensions

Analogies In Literature Mural

Invite students to choose a favorite book or story. Help the students find analogies within the story, such as nice to mean characters, characters to settings, or characters to problems. Then encourage students to make a large mural of the associations they come up with. Display the mural in the classroom.

Acting Out Analogies with Paper Plate Masks

Invite children to choose fairy tales or other favorite stories, such as "Little Red Riding Hood" and "Hansel and Gretel." Provide paper plates for the children and have them create masks of the main characters of each story. Then encourage children to create scenes illustrating the analogous relationships. For example, Little Red Riding Hood is to the big, bad wolf as Hansel and Gretel are to the witch.

Analogy Race

Divide the class into groups. Give each group the same list of familiar vocabulary words that can be used as analogies for one another. Then challenge the students to come up with a number of analogies using the words on the list. The first group to use all the words is the winner. Have the winning team share all of their analogies with the rest of the class.

Skill 8: Completing Word Relationships (Analogies)

Student's Name _____

Assessment Tool Progress Report

Progress

Improvement

Comments

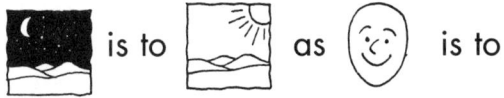

Skill 8: Completing Word Relationships (Analogies)

Name _____

Practice 1

All of the pictures in the large box are used as answers.

Example: cat is to kitten as dog is to puppy

1. night is to day as 🙂 is to

2. man is to girl as man is to

3. cow is to steak as pig is to

4. man is to woman as king is to

5. baby is to food as car is to

125

Skill 8: Completing Word Relationships (Analogies)

Name _____

Practice 2

All of the pictures in the large box are used as answers.

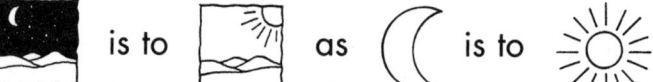

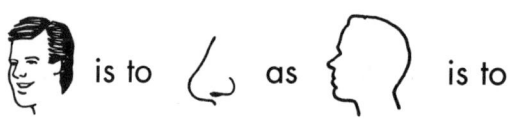

Example: [night scene] is to [day scene] as [moon] is to [sun]

1. [teacher at board] is to [book] as [nurse] is to ____

2. [rooster] is to [chick] as [deer] is to ____

3. [man's head] is to [nose] as [head silhouette] is to ____

4. [bird] is to [wing] as [tree] is to ____

5. [night sky] is to [person in coat] as [rain] is to ____

© Fearon Teacher Aids FE7965
Reproducible

126

Skill 8: Completing Word Relationships (Analogies)

Name _____

Practice 3

All of the pictures in the large box are **not** used as answers.

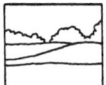

Example: ▢ is to 〰 as 🚗 is to 🚤

1. 👋 is to ⌚ as 👂 is to ____

2. 🏪 GROCERY is to 🍽 as 🏦 BANK is to ____

3. 🥕 is to 🫒 as 🍐 is to ____

4. 🍇 is to 📦 RAISINS as 🫒 is to ____

127

© Fearon Teacher Aids FE7965
Reproducible

Skill 8: Completing Word Relationships (Analogies)

Name _____

Practice 4

All of the pictures in the box are **not** used as answers.

Example: hand is to mitten as head is to hat

1.  tricycle is to wheels as bicycle is to

2. landscape is to train as sky is to

3.  bird is to feather as tree is to

4. bird is to worm as horse is to

© Fearon Teacher Aids FE7965
Reproducible

128

Name _____

Practice 5

All of the pictures in the box are used as answers.

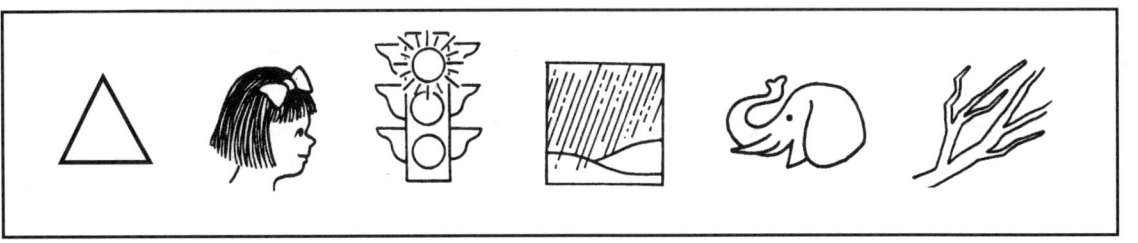

Example: Man is to 🧑‍🦰 as boy is to 👧

1. Go is to 🚦 as stop is to

2. Face is to 👃 as tree is to

3. Round is to ⭕ as pointed is to

4. Lion is to 🦁 as elephant is to

5. Dry is to ☀️ as wet is to

129

Skill 8: Completing Word Relationships (Analogies)

Name _____

Practice 6

All of the pictures in the box are **not** used as answers.

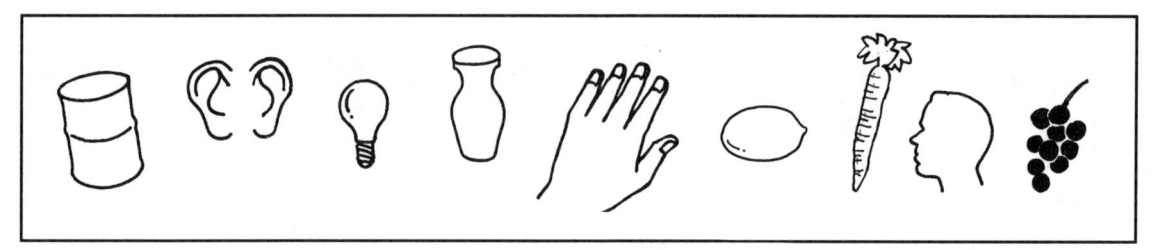

Example: Fruit is to 🍐 as vegetable is to 🥕

1. See is to 👁️ 👁️ as hear is to

2. Walk is to 👣 as hold is to

3. Sweet is to 🍭 as sour is to

4. Book is to 📄 as lamp is to

5. Milk is to 🥛 as oil is to

© Fearon Teacher Aids FE7965
Reproducible

Skill 8: Completing Word Relationships (Analogies)

Name _____

Practice 7

All of the words in the box are used as answers.

| write | quack | beet | yellow | finger | plane |

Example: 🍎 is to 🍇 as 🥕 is to   beet.

1. 〰️ is to boat as ☁️ is to _____.

2. 🐕 is to bark as 🦆 is to _____.

3. 💍 is to ear as 👁️ is to _____.

4. ☁️ is to blue as ☀️ is to _____.

5. 🥄 is to eat as ✏️ is to _____.

131

© Fearon Teacher Aids FE7965
Reproducible

Skill 8: Completing Word Relationships (Analogies)

Name _____

Practice 8

All of the words in the box are **not** used as answers.

tires	tall	whoo	bray	quack	tame
mean	small	dig	hole	house	building
church	ten	fifty	hundred	egg	

Example: 🐄 is to milk as 🐓 is to <u>egg</u>.

1.  🐖 is to oink as 🦉 is to _____.

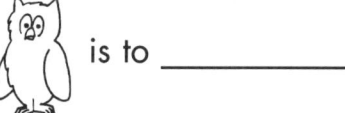

2.  👨‍⚕️ is to hospital as 👨 is to _____.

3.  🐅 is to wild as 🐕 is to _____.

4.  🪙 is to five as 💵 is to _____.

5. 🪚 is to cut as 🔨 is to _____.

© Fearon Teacher Aids FE7965
Reproducible

Skill 8: Completing Word Relationships (Analogies)

Name _____

Practice 9

Directions: Below are sets of words that have a certain relationship to one another. Each set has a missing word that you need to supply. Look at the first pair of words. Try to figure out what the relationship is. Then choose a word from the word list that best completes the second pair in the set. All the words in the word list are used as answers. The first is done for you.

Word List: sentence, wolf, bed, story, knee, smell

1. Sit is to chair as lie is to _____bed_____ .

2. Mouth is to taste as nose is to _____ .

3. Water is to shark as land is to _____ .

4. Arm is to leg as elbow is to _____ .

5. Sentence is to word as paragraph is to _____ .

6. Sentence is to paragraph as paragraph is to _____ .

Skill 8: Completing Word Relationships (Analogies)

Name _____

Practice 10

Directions: Below are sets of words that have a certain relationship to one another. Each set has a missing word that you need to supply. Look at the first pair of words. Try to figure out what the relationship is. Then choose a word from the word list that best completes the second pair in the set. All the words in the word list are **not** used as answers. The first is done for you.

Word List: hide, house, nice, proud, bull, hay, sow, stallion, ewe, gander, drake, stable, water, milk, drink, cruel, tired, great, hot

1. Bird is to nest as horse is to _____stable_____.

2. Cool is to cold as warm is to _____.

3. Cow is to bull as duck is to _____.

4. Deer is to doe as pig is to _____.

5. Hungry is to eat as thirsty is to _____.

6. In is to out as kind is to _____.

Skill 8: Completing Word Relationships (Analogies)

Name _____

Practice 11

Directions: Below are sets of words that have a certain relationship to one another. Each set has a missing word that you need to supply. Look at the first pair of words. Try to figure out what the relationship is. Then choose a word from the word list that best completes the second pair in the set. All the words in the word list are used as answers.

Word List: quiet, less, bean, cub, doe, always, yesterday, soft, young, weak

1. Night is to day as old is to _____.

2. Fruit is to plum as vegetable is to _____.

3. Black is to white as hard is to _____.

4. Cat is to kitten as bear is to _____.

5. Horse is to mare as deer is to _____.

6. Loud is to soft as noisy is to _____.

7. Wrong is to right as never is to _____.

8. Stop is to go as strong is to _____.

9. Most is to least as more is to _____.

10. Tomorrow is to today as today is to _____.

Skill 8: Completing Word Relationships (Analogies)

Name _____

Practice 12

Directions: Below are sets of words that have a certain relationship to one another. Each set has a missing word that you need to supply. Look at the first pair of words. Try to figure out what the relationship is. Then choose a word from the word list that best completes the second pair in the set. All the words in the word list are used as answers.

Word List: nephew, buy, dollar, wheel, low, empty, eat, drake, toe, neigh

1. Up is to down as high is to _____.

2. Hand is to finger as foot is to _____.

3. Sister is to brother as niece is to _____.

4. Donkey is to bray as horse is to _____.

5. Chicken is to rooster as duck is to _____.

6. Penny is to dime as dime is to _____.

7. In is to out as sell is to _____.

8. Sit is to stand as full is to _____.

9. Milk is to drink as food is to _____.

10. Car is to tire as wagon is to _____.

© Fearon Teacher Aids FE7965
Reproducible

Skill 8: Completing Word Relationships (Analogies)

Name _____

Practice 13

Directions: Below are sets of words that have a certain relationship to one another. Each set has a missing word that you need to supply. Look at the first pair of words. Try to figure out what the relationship is. Then choose a word from the word list that best completes the second pair in the set. All the words in the word list are **not** used as answers.

Word List: silk, vehicle, clothing, cold, eight, ten, cool, small, seven, moon, star, nickel, dime, dollar, quarter, dumb, lemon, even, wool, sour

1. Happy is to sad as hot is to _____.

2. Right is to wrong as odd is to _____.

3. Awake is to asleep as smart is to _____.

4. Sweet is to sour as candy is to _____.

5. Pliers is to tool as ship is to _____.

6. Quarter is to half-dollar as half-dollar is to _____.

7. Earth is to planet as sun is to _____.

8. Meat is to food as dress is to _____.

9. Bee is to honey as worm is to _____.

10. Fly is to six as spider is to _____.

137

© Fearon Teacher Aids FE7965
Reproducible

Skill 8: Completing Word Relationships (Analogies)

Name _____

Practice 14

Directions: Below are sets of words that have a certain relationship to one another. Each set has a missing word that you need to supply. Look at the first pair of words. Try to figure out what the relationship is. Then choose a word from the word list that best completes the second pair in the set. All the words in the word list are **not** used as answers.

Word List: sibling, child, nephew, niece, sister, city, depot, six, four, two, continent, thirsty, water, drink, mildew, talk, shout, hangar, excuse, tell, help, protect, mouse, ant, turtle, tired, rough, Africa

1. Car is to garage as plane is to _____.

2. Uncle is to aunt as brother is to _____.

3. China is to Asia as Egypt is to _____.

4. Triangle is to three as square is to _____.

5. Cotton is to soft as sandpaper is to _____.

6. Nap is to sleep as sip is to _____.

7. Friend is to pal as pardon is to _____.

8. Drizzle is to downpour as whisper is to _____.

9. Warm-blooded is to seal as cold-blooded is to _____.

10. Moisture is to rust as fungus is to _____.

Name _____

Practice 15

Directions: Below are sets of words that have a certain relationship to one another. Each set has a missing word that you need to supply. Look at the first pair of words. Try to figure out what the relationship is. Then choose a word from the word list that best completes the second pair in the set. All the words in the word list are **not** used as answers.

Word List: mister, sir, clothing, triangle, one, reverend, pupil, sleep, look, bite, Africa, South America, country, few, clean, tomorrow, today, before, still, two, six, four, feet, toes, Asia, city, yesterday, Sunday, Monday

1. Good is to bad as dirty is to _____.

2. Robin is to two as deer is to _____.

3. France is to Europe as Japan is to _____.

4. Country is to continent as state is to _____.

5. Ambassador is to Honorable as minister is to _____.

6. Present is to now as past is to _____.

7. One is to three as yard is to _____.

8. Quiver is to arrow as suitcase is to _____.

9. Finger is to nail as eye is to _____.

10. Today is to yesterday as tomorrow is to _____.

Skill 9:
Finding Inconsistencies

Explanation

Good thinkers are logical—that is, they are able to reason correctly. Finding inconsistencies refers to statements that do not make sense—they are illogical and not in accord with the given information. Finding inconsistencies in text is an important skill for students to learn. This skill helps students be alert while reading, learn to think logically, and question what they read.

Teaching Strategies in Action

Good readers are alert readers. Help your students recognize that everything that they read is not necessarily true or correct. If they read something that does not make sense, even if it is a textbook written by an authority in the field, they should question it.

Example:

If, in a book about Mexico, students found the statement, "There are approximately 10,000 people in Mexico City," should they believe it? Ask the students to reread the sentence. Does it make sense? Mexico City is the capital of Mexico. Ten thousand people is not really a lot of people living in a capital city. No, it doesn't make sense. They must have meant 10,000,000.

Sample Practices

Here are some sample practices that you can use with your students.

1. The dog meowed at the mail carrier.

   This sentence is inconsistent. A dog doesn't meow. The writer must have meant "the dog barked."

2. New York City is the capital of the state of New York.
   The writer must have meant to write "Albany" instead of "New York City."

3. Ms. Jacob has 30 children in her park. At 2:30, all the children ran out to play in the class.

   This sentence does not make sense. If re-read, one can see that the words "park" and "class" were switched. The sentence should read:

   Ms. Jacob has 30 children in her class. At 2:30, all the children ran out to play in the park.

Modeling Strategy

Here is how Ms. Evans, using a modeling strategy, helps her students recognize that good readers are alert readers.

Ms. Evans writes the following statement on the chalkboard:

Humans drink about 1,000 quarts of liquid in a week.

Ms. Evans asks her students to read the statement. Then she says, "When I read this statement, it doesn't make sense to me. I keep re-reading it because I think I have not read it correctly. I decide that the writer must have made a mistake. It doesn't make sense to me because I know there are only seven days in a week. Even if someone drank four quarts of liquid a day, which is a very large amount, that person would still only be drinking 28 quarts. I know that there are four large glasses of liquid in one quart. That means I would have to drink 16 large glasses of liquids in one day. That would be hard to do. But even if I were to do that, I still would only be drinking 28 quarts a week. To drink 1,000 quarts would mean I would be drinking 4,000 large glasses of liquid a week. That does not make any sense. The '1,000' is a mistake. The writer probably meant to say 10 quarts."

Ms. Evans then writes the following sentence on the chalkboard. She asks the children to read it and tell her what they think about it.

The tame lion attacked the three men.

"Does it make sense to you?" she asks. "When I read the sentence," she continues, "it doesn't make sense to me because a tame lion would most likely not attack anyone. The writer probably meant to say *wild*. A wild animal would more likely attack people."

Learning Objective

To find inconsistencies in sentences or paragraphs and replace these with the correct word or words.

Directions for Student Practices

Use the student practices on pages 144–148 to help your students acquire, reinforce, and review finding inconsistencies. Pick and choose the practices based on the needs and developmental levels of your students. Answers for the student practice pages are on page 175.

When practicing finding inconsistencies, have the children read the directions and then answer the questions. For those who have difficulty reading, read the directions aloud to the children and orally ask them the questions.

Extensions

Sing a Simple Song

Invite the children to sing some familiar songs with you, such as "Twinkle, Twinkle, Little Star" or "Mary Had a Little Lamb." As you sing with the children, change one of the words in the chorus. The children will, of course, notice your blunder. Then ask the children to tell you the correct word.

Making Posters

Encourage students to find errors in stories, books, magazine articles, headlines, and so on. If possible, keep a small list of errors yourself. Once errors have been found, help students determine how the meanings of the sentences or paragraphs are changed by the errors. Then invite students to make posters of especially funny or absurd errors.

Changing Titles

Invite students to choose some of their favorite books or stories. Encourage children to change one word in each of the story titles that radically changes the meaning of the title into something funny or ridiculous. Students can then make-up stories to go with their new titles.

Skill 9: Finding Inconsistencies

Student's Name _____

Assessment Tool Progress Report

Progress

Improvement

Comments

Skill 9: Finding Inconsistencies

Name _____

Practice 1

Directions: Read each sentence carefully. Find the word in each sentence that does not make sense. Replace that word with one from the word list that does make sense in the sentence. All the words in the word list are **not** used as answers.

Word List: night, bread, cold, hot, slippery, feathers, bones, falls, rises, stays

1. The ice was dry, so I fell. _____

2. We had to pluck the scales off the chicken. _____

3. The stars lit up the sky at noon. _____

4. We like to eat bead and jam. _____

5. In the morning, the sun sets. _____

Name _____

Practice 2

Directions: Read each sentence carefully. Find the word in each sentence that does not make sense. Replace that word with one from the word list that does make sense in the sentence. All the words in the word list are **not** used as answers.

Word List: bottom, day, half-dollars, nickels, quarters, dusk, western, mine, cow, beard

1. I live in the eastern part of town, and my brother lives opposite me in the northern part of town. _____

2. At dawn, the sun sets. _____

3. The farmer milks the crow every morning. _____

4. My father gave me four dimes, which were just enough to buy one dollar's worth of paper and pencils. _____

5. His bear had grown so long that we did not know who he was. _____

145

© Fearon Teacher Aids FE7965
Reproducible

Skill 9: Finding Inconsistencies

Skill 9: Finding Inconsistencies

Name _____

Practice 3

Directions: Read each sentence carefully. Find the word in each sentence that does not make sense. Replace that word with one from the word list that does make sense in the sentence. All the words in the word list are **not** used as answers.

Word List: five, stag, sow, sugar, fine, wild, tender, three, chicks, pepper, doe

1. My mother won't let me have any tame pets. _____

2. The hen looked proudly at her newborn ducklings. _____

3. The mare led her deer family to safety. _____

4. He put salt on his food to make it sweeter. _____

5. At school, we always line up to go home when the clock strikes thee. _____

© Fearon Teacher Aids FE7965
Reproducible

146

Name _____

Practice 4

Directions: Read the short story carefully. Underline the words in the story that do not make sense. Choose words from the word list to replace the words that do not make sense. All the words in the word list are used as answers.

Word List: noisy, rooster, on, farm, five, morning, hen, crowing

A duck, a rooster, a hen, and five chicks lived together. They lived in a barn on a jungle. They stayed together all the time. Every evening, the hen would awaken everyone by blowing, "Cock-a-doodle-doo." The rooster would spend a lot of her time sitting in the eggs. The duck would play with the three chicks. It was always very quiet in the barn because they were always chattering.

1. _____ 5. _____

2. _____ 6. _____

3. _____ 7. _____

4. _____ 8. _____

Skill 9: Finding Inconsistencies

Name _____

Practice 5

Directions: Read the short story carefully. Underline the words in the story that do not make sense. Choose words from the word list to replace the words that do not make sense. All the words in the word list are used as answers. (If a word appears twice in the word list it means it is used twice.)

Word List: stopped, three, Mrs., her, stopped, kind, loud, sunny, noon, sun, Many

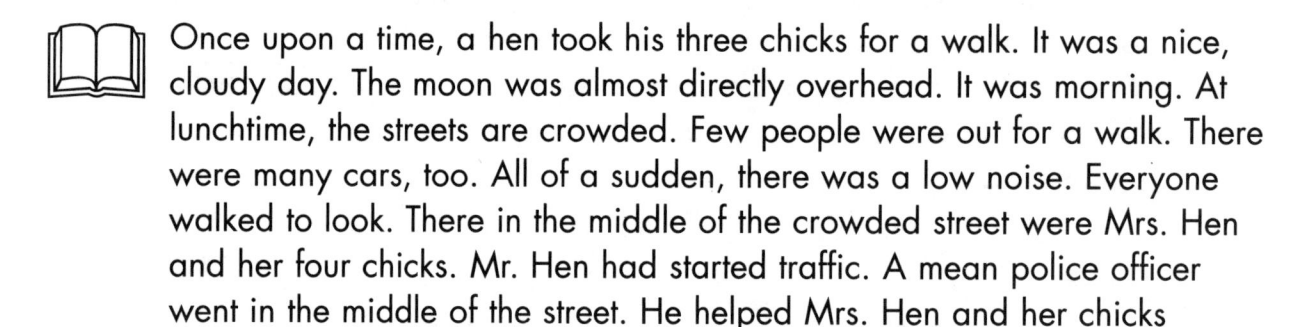

Once upon a time, a hen took his three chicks for a walk. It was a nice, cloudy day. The moon was almost directly overhead. It was morning. At lunchtime, the streets are crowded. Few people were out for a walk. There were many cars, too. All of a sudden, there was a low noise. Everyone walked to look. There in the middle of the crowded street were Mrs. Hen and her four chicks. Mr. Hen had started traffic. A mean police officer went in the middle of the street. He helped Mrs. Hen and her chicks cross the street.

1. _____   6. _____

2. _____   7. _____

3. _____   8. _____

4. _____   9. _____

5. _____   10. _____

11. _____

Skill 10:
Distinguishing Between Fact and Opinion

Explanation

The ability to differentiate between fact and opinion is a very important skill that students need to develop. Often, opinions are presented as though they are facts. Opinions are not facts. They are based on attitudes or feelings. Opinions can vary from individual to individual—they cannot be proven right or wrong conclusively. Facts, on the other hand, do not change from person to person. Facts can be proven to be true.

Teaching Strategies in Action

It is important to help your students as early as possible to determine whether information is factual or not. Present a picture to the children and ask them if they like it. After a number of children in the class have given their opinions, discuss with them how different children have different feelings about the picture. Point out to the children that they were giving their opinions about the picture and opinions may change from person to person.

Next, ask one child to tell you his or her name. Then call on other children in the class to give the name of that same child. Discuss with the children how everyone agrees on the child's name. Explain to the children that it's a fact that Mary Smith's name is Mary Smith. Tell children that something that is a fact does not change from person to person. Facts can be proven to be true.

Example:

Facts	**Opinions**
Albany is the capital of New York.	That is a pretty dress.
Twelve inches equals a foot.	He is very smart.
A meter equals 39.37 inches.	It's important to visit museums.

Sample Practices

Here are some sample practices that you can use with your students.
1. He has a nice smile. (opinion)
2. This chocolate cake tastes great! (opinion)
3. A horse has four legs. (fact)
4. All people are mammals. (fact)
5. I can call my friends on the telephone. (fact)
6. That clown's red nose makes him look silly. (opinion)

Modeling Strategy

Mrs. Brown presents the children with the following sentences. She tells the children that she will show them how she figures out whether something is a fact or an opinion.

> Melissa is pretty.
> Andrew is a good ball player.
> The United States is a country.
> Arithmetic is a school subject.
> Baseball is fun.
> Monday is a day of the week.
> Ice cream tastes good.
> Frank is a nice guy.

"I know," Mrs. Brown says, "that when something is an opinion, it can change from person to person. It cannot be proven to be right or wrong. If something is a fact, it does not change from person to person. It can be proven or shown to be true."

"When I read the statement, 'Melissa is pretty,' I know the statement is an opinion because not everyone will agree with me. What I think is pretty, someone else may not think is pretty. Also, the statement 'Andrew is a good ball player' is an opinion. Even though I think he is a good ball player, not everyone agrees. It is my opinion. However, the sentence that says 'The United States is a country' is not an opinion. I know that statement is a fact. It can be proven to be true. Everyone agrees. We can all find information or evidence to prove it," says Mrs. Brown.

Mrs. Brown then goes over all the other sentences with the students and asks them to tell her whether each sentence is a fact or an opinion.

Learning Objective

To determine the difference between fact and opinion.

Directions for Student Practices

Use the student practices on pages 153–157 to help your students acquire, reinforce, and review distinguishing between fact and opinion. Pick and choose the practices based on the needs and developmental levels of your students. Answers for the student practice pages are on page 175.

When practicing distinguishing between fact and opinion, have the children read the directions and then answer the questions. For those who have difficulty reading, read the directions aloud to the children and orally ask them the questions.

Extensions

Bulletin Board

Make a "Fact or Opinion" bulletin-board display. Divide a bulletin board into two sections—one titled "Fact" and the other titled "Opinion." As students come across statements of fact or opinion in their reading, encourage students to write the statements on strips of paper. Then invite children to place the statements on the appropriate side of the bulletin board.

Character Containers

Invite children to choose a favorite book or story. As you read the story together with the class, have children keep track of the characters' opinions throughout the story. Write the opinions of each character on the chalkboard. Then give each child a covered oatmeal container and his or her choice of construction paper. Each child can draw the face of one of the characters on the lid of the oatmeal container. Help each child write that character's opinions on the construction paper and then glue the paper around the containers. Display the character containers in the classroom.

Book Reports

When the students are reading nonfiction and fiction books or stories, challenge students to list five of the most important facts they learned from their reading, as well as list five opinions that were stated in the book or story. You may want to provide book report forms for the children to fill out as they read.

Skill 10: Distinguishing Between Fact and Opinion

Student's Name _____

Assessment Tool Progress Report

Progress

Improvement

Comments

© Fearon Teacher Aids FE7965
Reproducible

Skill 10: Distinguishing Between Fact and Opinion

Name _____

Practice 1

Directions: Read each sentence carefully. Decide if the statement is a fact or if the statement is an opinion. Remember that if the statement is an opinion, then it can change from person to person. If the statement is a fact, it can't change. In front of each sentence, put the letter **O** if it's an opinion and the letter **F** if it's a fact.

_____ 1. That picture is pretty.

_____ 2. Parents work hard.

_____ 3. Baseball is fun to play.

_____ 4. Spelling is a school subject.

_____ 5. An apple is a fruit.

© Fearon Teacher Aids FE7965
Reproducible

Skill 10: Distinguishing Between Fact and Opinion

Name _____

Practice 2

Directions: Read each sentence carefully. Decide if the statement is a fact or if the statement is an opinion. Remember that if the statement is an opinion, then it can change from person to person. If the statement is a fact, it can't change. In front of each sentence, put the letter **O** if it's an opinion and the letter **F** if it's a fact.

_____ 1. Math is a hard subject.

_____ 2. Milk is a dairy product.

_____ 3. Sixty minutes equals an hour.

_____ 4. This room is too hot.

_____ 5. Kelsey is a good singer.

Skill 10: Distinguishing Between Fact and Opinion

Name _____

Practice 3

Directions: Read each sentence carefully. Decide if the statement is a fact or if the statement is an opinion. Remember that if the statement is an opinion, then it can change from person to person. If the statement is a fact, it can't change. In front of each sentence, put the letter **O** if it's an opinion and the letter **F** if it's a fact.

_____   1. A turtle is able to live on land.

_____   2. Turtles are fun to own.

_____   3. Turtles are ugly.

_____   4. A turtle has a bony shell.

_____   5. A turtle is able to live in fresh water.

Skill 10: Distinguishing Between Fact and Opinion

Name _____

Practice 4

Directions: Read each sentence carefully. Decide if the statement is a fact or if the statement is an opinion. Remember that if the statement is an opinion, then it can change from person to person. If the statement is a fact, it can't change. In front of each sentence, put the letter **O** if it's an opinion and the letter **F** if it's a fact.

_____ 1. Television is fun to watch.

_____ 2. Game shows are better than talk shows.

_____ 3. A person can't fly like a bird.

_____ 4. Jogging is the best exercise.

_____ 5. Air is needed to live.

Skill 10: Distinguishing Between Fact and Opinion

Name _____

Practice 5

Directions: Read each sentence carefully. Decide if the statement is a fact or if the statement is an opinion. Remember that if the statement is an opinion, then it can change from person to person. If the statement is a fact, it can't change. In front of each sentence, put the letter **O** if it's an opinion and the letter **F** if it's a fact.

_____   1. Ice is frozen water.

_____   2. History books are fun to read.

_____   3. Food is needed in order to live.

_____   4. Lemons taste good.

_____   5. Fairy tales are fun to read.

Skill 11:
Using Divergent Thinking

Explanation

Divergent thinking has to do with the many different ways of looking at things. The dictionary defines the word *divergent* as "differing from the standard." In other words, divergent thinkers are those who can look at things differently or in a more creative way. Good divergent thinkers are able to look beyond the obvious and come up with new or alternate solutions. Students should be encouraged to try to solve problems in many different ways and be intelligent risk-takers and make educated guesses.

Teaching Strategies in Action

Help your students recognize that divergent thinking requires that they go beyond the obvious and look for alternate ways to solve problems. Children need to know that they can look at things in many different ways. By "differing from the standard," they are not only being more creative, but this will help them solve problems and think things through in different ways.

Help children be more divergent thinkers with the following brainstorming activity:

Example:

Ask your students to state the many different uses of a brick. You should expect answers such as the following:

A brick can be used to build a wall.
A brick can be used as a bed warmer.
A brick can be used to write with.
A brick can be carved out and used as a bowl.
A brick can be used as a paperweight.
And so on...

If your students state only uses that include building, encourage the children to be more creative thinkers by going beyond the obvious uses of a brick. The most creative is to come up with some unique uses for bricks, such as some of the uses listed above. During brainstorming activities, encourage children to build on one another's ideas—anything goes. After the brainstorming session, take the time to talk about and evaluate the answers with the children.

Sample Practices

Here are some sample practices that you can use with your students:

1. Ask the children what they could do with one mitten. Some of the answers could be:
   Wear the mitten on one hand and keep the other hand in your pocket.
   Make a puppet out of the mitten.
   Wear the mitten on your nose as a nose warmer.
   Carry your pencils in the mitten.
   Use the mitten as a cup warmer.
   Unravel the mitten and knit a cap.

2. Read the following paragraph with your students. Invite students to answer the questions that follow:

Zach and Eric decided to go on a hike. They put on their hiking boots and set off on their hike. They hiked for a long time. Finally, they came to a huge mountain. In the side of the mountain was a dark cave. Zach looked inside. "Should we go in?" he asked Eric. Eric shook his head.

Questions:
1. Do you think Eric wanted to go into the cave? Why or why not?
2. What do you think was in the cave?
3. How do you think the story will end?

Modeling Strategy

Here is how Mr. Jackson models for his students how to answer divergent-thinking questions. He has the children read the following short selection and then the questions that follow the story.

Zip and Zap, a cat and rat who live on the moon, had just received new space suits. They wanted to try them out. They put on their suits and went outside. They floated and floated far away. Zip and Zap were so excited about their new suits that they didn't notice where they were going. "Zip, where are we?" asked Zap. "I don't know," replied Zip, "I was following you."

Questions:
1. What do you think Zip and Zap are going to do?

2. What do you think the suits look like? Draw a picture of one of the suits.

3. Write an ending to this story.

Mr. Jackson says, "I just read the short story. I see from the story that Zip and Zap are so excited about their new suits that they are not thinking about anything else. While I was reading the story, I felt that this will probably get them into trouble. I wonder if their parents know they left. I wonder if anyone knows they are outside. This can be scary if it gets late.

"If I were Zip and Zap, I would try to find something familiar to help me figure out where I was. I picture the suits to be silver with large plastic domes for the heads. On the suits, there are lots of buttons. If I were Zip or Zap wearing one of the suits, I would press each button. Maybe one is a special remote control phone. In my ending, I would have Zip and Zap floating around until they are very tired. Then they would start pressing each button on their suits. One of the buttons would connect them to the control center in the large air-filled dome in which they live. Then Zip and Zap would hear voices on the other end. The cat and rat in charge would tell Zip and Zap which button to push so someone could guide them home."

Mr. Jackson then says to the children, "Did you notice that I used the information from the story to write the ending? My ending has to make sense and relate to the story. Now, I want each of you to try to write an ending for the story."

Encourage children to share their new endings to the story. Ask each child who is sharing to go through what his or her thinking process was for the new ending.

Learning Objective

To go beyond the text to answer questions that require divergent thinking.

Directions for Student Practices

Use the student practices on pages 163–167 to help your students acquire, reinforce, and review divergent thinking. Pick and choose the practices based on the needs and developmental levels of your students. Answers for the student practice pages are on page 175.

When practicing divergent thinking, have the children read the story and then answer the questions. For those who have difficulty reading, read the story aloud to the children and orally ask them the questions.

Extensions

Write a New Ending or Sequel

Invite children to write new endings to a favorite story. Children can write or dictate the new endings and also illustrate the new endings to the stories. Or, challenge the children to write sequels to favorite stories, such as " 'Married Life' by Cinderella" or "Whatever Happened to the Three Little Pigs?"

Add a Character

Divide the class into small groups. Invite each group to choose a situation from a favorite story. Encourage the children in each group to role play the character or characters. Then challenge the children to add a new character to the story and see how the situation changes. All the groups can role play their new situations for the rest of the class.

New Settings

Have children rewrite or retell familiar stories with different settings, such as the desert, the Arctic, or the moon. Encourage children to also illustrate the different story settings.

What Would You Do?

Encourage students to keep journals of their thoughts and ideas as they are reading stories or books. Ask each student to include in his or her journal how they would solve a particular problem differently from the way a character in the story they are reading would. Invite students to share their ideas with the class, if they wish.

Advice Column

Ask students to role play characters from a favorite story that have a particular problem. Students, in the role of the story characters, can write letters to an advice columnist asking for help in solving their problems. Students can switch letters and play the role of advice columnist by answering the letters and helping the particular characters solve their problems.

Skill 11: Using Divergent Thinking

Student's Name _____

Assessment Tool Progress Report

Progress

Improvement

Comments

Skill 11: Using Divergent Thinking

Name _____

Practice 1

Directions: Read the make-believe story about Zip and Zap, an imaginary cat and rat who live on the moon. Answer the questions following the story.

One day, Zip and Zap were very excited. They had just heard some good news. Their Earth cousins were coming to visit them. They were coming on the space shuttle. Their Earth cousins had never been to the moon. "What fun we will have," said Zap to Zip. "I wonder what we should plan to do," said Zip. "I wonder how long they will stay," said Zap. "I wonder what we can give them as a present," said Zip. "Let's make something that is special," said Zap. "Good idea," said Zap. "Let's do it now."

1. What do you think Zip and Zap look like? Describe each one:

   _____

   _____

   _____

2. What do you think Zip and Zap's cousins look like? Describe them:

   _____

   _____

   _____

3. What kind of games do you think Zip and Zap will play with their cousins?_____

   _____

4. What do you think Zip and Zap will make for their cousins?

   _____

   _____

5. What presents do you think Zip and Zap's cousins may bring for Zip and Zap? _____

   _____

163

© Fearon Teacher Aids FE7965
Reproducible

Skill 11: Using Divergent Thinking

Name _____

Practice 2

Directions: Read the make-believe story about Zip and Zap, an imaginary cat and rat who live on the moon. Answer the questions following the story.

One day, Zip and Zap decided that they would try to see the "Big One." Zip and Zap had heard the older cats and rats talk about the "Big One." The older cats and rats said that no one had ever seen the "Big One." Well, Zip and Zap would try. Zip and Zap put on their outdoor clothes and went in search of the "Big One." They walked and walked. Then they walked some more. Finally, Zap said, "Let's stop and take a nap." So Zip and Zap took a nap. When Zip and Zap took a nap, they dreamed about the "Big One." When Zip and Zap got up from their nap, they felt as if they had seen the "Big One."

1. What do you think the "Big One" is?

   _____

   _____

2. What do you think Zip's and Zap's dreams about the "Big One" were?

   _____

   _____

3. What do you think the "Big One" looks like?

   _____

   _____

4. What do you think Zip and Zap will do next?

   _____

   _____

© Fearon Teacher Aids FE7965
Reproducible

Skill 11: Using Divergent Thinking

Name _____

Practice 3

Directions: Read the short story. Answer the questions following the story.

Zeres lives in the forest. Zeres is a troll. Only animals in the forest can see trolls. Forest trolls usually come out at night and sleep during the day. Zeres is a special kind of troll. Zeres likes to play with children. The other trolls do not want Zeres to play with children. Children are not supposed to be able to see trolls. No human beings are supposed to be able to see trolls. Only the animals can see trolls.

This, however, does not stop Zeres. Every day when the other trolls are asleep, Zeres sneaks out. Zeres skips through the forest in search of children. When Zeres sees a child, Zeres claps, jumps up and down three times, and screams with glee.

The children like to play with Zeres. Zeres knows lots of fun things to do. Zeres also knows lots of things and takes the children to lots of places. Sometimes they go to the tops of mountains. Sometimes they go to deserts. Sometimes they go on a ship. Sometimes they fly to another land. The children love Zeres. Zeres is their best friend.

1. Do you think Zeres is a boy or girl? Why?

   _____
   _____

2. Describe Zeres. What do you think Zeres looks like?

   _____
   _____

3. Make up an adventure that Zeres has with some children.

   _____
   _____
   _____
   _____

© Fearon Teacher Aids FE7965
Reproducible

Skill 11: Using Divergent Thinking

Name _____

Practice 4

Directions: Read the short story. Answer the questions following the story. Use another sheet of paper if you need more space to write.

A young man went to bed after eating a very big supper. While he was sleeping, he had a dream. He dreamed that he had gone for a walk. While walking, he stepped on a sharp nail. The dream was so real that the young man awakened. When he awakened, he rushed to put a bandage on his foot. He then went back to sleep. The next day, the young man went to town. His friend asked him why he was limping. The young man told him what had happened. His friend said, "I have a good idea. The next time you go to sleep, wear your sandals." The young man listened to his friend. From then on, he wore his sandals to bed.

1. Make up another dream that the young man has.

   _____

   _____

2. Make up a silly dream that the young man has.

   _____

   _____

3. Make up another ending for the story.

   _____

   _____

4. Write about a dream that you have had.

   _____

   _____

© Fearon Teacher Aids FE7965
Reproducible

Skill 11: Using Divergent Thinking

Name _____

Practice 5

Directions: Read the short story. Answer the questions following the story.

Once upon a time there was a princess who believed everything she heard. This princess was a very nice person. Her only problem was that she believed everything anyone said to her. If you told her that the moon was made of cheese, she would believe you. She would also ask for a slice of it. If you told her that you could pick the stars and use them for lights, she would believe you. She would also ask for a star.

The king didn't know what to do. He loved his daughter, but he was upset about her problem. "What will happen when I am gone? She will believe anything. I must get her to say that something is not true," thought the king. The king had an idea. He called his advisers. He told them that he would give one wish to the person who would make the princess say, "That is a lie."

People from all over tried to make the princess say, "That is a lie." They made up silly stories, but the princess believed all of them. One day, a poor country boy came to talk to the princess. He said to her that he had seen her father, the king, in his town and that her father would not give any money or help to the people in his town. The princess looked at him. Her face turned red. She screamed, "That is a lie. My father always helps people." "That's true," said the poor country boy. "Now, I have only one wish. I wish that you would marry me. "The princess thought that was a nice idea. The king did, too. So the princess and the poor country boy were married and lived happily together.

1. Make up a silly story that the princess believes.

   _____
   _____
   _____

2. Make up another ending for the story.

   _____
   _____
   _____

© Fearon Teacher Aids FE7965
Reproducible

Diagnostic Checklist for Selected Reading Comprehension Skills

Student's Name:

Grade:

Teacher:

	YES	NO
1. The student is able to state the meaning of a word in context.		
2. The student is able to give the meaning of a phrase or a clause in a sentence.		
3. The student is able to give the meaning of a sentence in a paragraph.		
4. The student is able to recall information that is explicitly stated in the passage (literal-type questions).		
5. The student is able to state the main idea of the paragraph.		
6. The student is able to state details to support the main idea of a paragraph.		
7. The student can state cause/effect relationships.		
8. The student is able to answer a question that requires "reading between the lines."		
9. The student is able to draw a conclusion from what is read.		
10. The student can complete analogy proportions.		
11. The student can hypothesize the author's purpose for writing the selection.		
12. The student can differentiate between fact and opinion.		
13 The student can differentiate between fantasy and reality.		
14. The student can go beyond the text to come up with alternative solutions or ways to end a story or solve a problem in the selection.		
15. The student shows that he or she enjoys reading by voluntarily choosing to read.		

© Fearon Teacher Aids FE7965
Reproducible

Answers

Answers to Skill 1

Practice 1 (p. 25)
1. Zip
2. Zap
3. on the moon
4. play
5. cats and rats

Practice 2 (p. 26)
1. all the cats and rats
2. a very large house
3. special air masks
4. air
5. laugh

Practice 3 (p. 27)
1. happy
2. as soon as daylight came
3. their Earth cousins
4. on the space shuttle
5. no

Practice 4 (p. 28)
1. to the library
2. to take out some books on the planet Earth and see pictures of the Earth
3. a brightly lit, round room
4. in the middle of the large house
5. books about the Earth
6. went to the letter *E*, found the word *Earth*, pressed a button
7. pictures of the Earth

Practice 5 (p. 29)
1. special clothing and air masks
2. on the space shuttle
3. their Earth cousins
4. funny
5. air masks
6. air masks
7. put on special Earth clothing
8. laugh

Answers to Skill 2

Practice 1 (p. 36)
1. No. It is stated that they are using the same water that the first cats and rats brought with them. They came from some other place that had water.
2. There is no water on the moon and water is needed to live.
3. Air and water are precious on the moon because the moon doesn't have any. Air and water are necessary to live.
4. Air and water.

Practice 2 (p. 37)
1. No. Zip and Zap wear their space clothes and air masks in the spaceship.
2. No. It is stated that the spaceship is the same one that brought Zip and Zap to the moon.
3. Yes. It is their means of travel. It is stated that there are special cats and rats who take care of the spaceship and that the spaceship is well taken care of.
4. Yes. Every month the school goes on a space trip.

Practice 3 (p. 38)
1. Zap was wearing the special outdoor clothing because he didn't float away when he jumped up. When Zip jumped up, he floated away.
2. He wasn't wearing the special clothing.
3. He floated away because he wasn't wearing special clothing.
4. No, because he forgot to put on his special outdoor clothing.

Practice 4 (p. 39)
Answers will vary. Listed are possible answers.
1. It's kind. (It saved Zip.)
2. It knows where Zip lives. (It brings Zip to his house.)
3. It knows why Zip floated away. (It calls Zip a "suitless wonder.")
4. It seems jolly and has a sense of humor. (It says, "Ho, ho, ho." It also calls Zip a "suitless wonder.")
5. It must be large. (It was able to grab Zip, who was floating high into space. Zip heard a booming voice, but Zip didn't see where it was coming from.)

Practice 5 (p. 40)
1. true
2. true
3. can't tell
4. true
5. false
6. can't tell
7. can't tell
8. can't tell
9. true
10. can't tell

Practice 6 (p. 41)
1. can't tell
2. true
3. true
4. true
5. false

Practice 7 (p. 42)
1. true
2. false
3. can't tell
4. can't tell
5. can't tell
6. can't tell
7. true
8. true
9. can't tell
10. can't tell

© Fearon Teacher Aids FE7965

Practice 8 (p. 43)
1. true
2. true
3. true
4. true
5. can't tell
6. can't tell
7. false
8. can't tell
9. can't tell
10. true

Practice 9 (p. 44)
1. false
2. true
3. false
4. true
5. can't tell
6. can't tell
7. true
8. can't tell

Practice 10 (p. 45)
Answers will vary.
1. They were lazy because they didn't bother to move the box out of the middle of the road. or They were not concerned that someone might trip over the box.
2. He didn't want to be seen and he wanted to see what the people would do when they saw the box.
3. The boy works hard. He is not lazy. He cares about other people. It said in the story that he moved the box away so that no one would trip on it.
4. Under the box.
5. The rich man.
6. The rich man wanted to find someone who wasn't lazy or was kind and reward that person. The person who went to the trouble of moving the box would find the gold.

Answers to Skill 3
Practice 1 (p. 51)
1. Today is a special day on the moon (effect); it is Children's Day (cause)
2. Zip and Zap love this day (effect); there are lots of parties (cause)
3. The parties are fun (effect); the children play lots of games (cause)
4. Funny clowns do lots of tricks (cause); the children laugh (effect)

Practice 2 (p. 52)
1. Zip and Zap ate too much (cause); they got stomachaches (effect)
2. The next day, they both had to stay home (effect); they did not feel well (cause)
3. They did not want to look at food (effect); it made them sick (cause)
4. Zip and Zap went to see the doctor (effect); their stomachs hurt so much (cause)

Practice 3 (p. 53)
1. Naomi and Phil didn't play outside for two days (effect); their dads said it was too cold (cause)
2. Phil has lots of games (cause); I want to visit him (effect)
3. It was no fun (effect); when it was too cold to play outside (cause)

Practice 4 (p. 54)
1. Karesha was bored (effect); she didn't have anything to do (cause)
2. Then she asked her mother what she could do (effect); she couldn't think of anything (cause)
3. Your brother knows you love to read (cause); he brought you lots of new books from the library (effect)
4. I like this one (effect); it is so funny (cause)

Practice 5 (p. 55)
1. Linda went with her family to Seattle (effect); she wanted to visit her cousins (cause)
2. I like school (effect); there are lots of things to do (cause)
3. I like to learn about things (cause); I like school (effect)
4. The children were all happy (effect); Burt and Linda came back to school (cause)
5. Burt and Linda are a lot of fun (cause); the other children missed them (effect)

Answers to Skill 4
Answers will vary.
Practice 1 (p. 62)
Main idea: Zip and Zap's birthdays are fun. (4)
Sample title: Zip and Zap's Birthday

Practice 2 (p. 63)
Main idea: Zip and Zap's first fight makes them feel sad. (3)
Sample title: Zip and Zap's First Fight

Practice 3 (p. 64)
Main idea: The moon's weather forces Zip and Zap to stay in their house. (5)
Sample title: The Moon's Weather

Practice 4 (p. 65)
Main idea: A new family becomes part of Beth's neighborhood
Sample title: The New Family in Beth's Neighborhood

Practice 5 (p. 66)
Main idea: Fiona decides to go to a birthday party after thinking about what new friends she might make.
Sample title: Fiona and the Birthday Party

Answers to Skill 5
Answers will vary.

Practice 1 (p. 73)
Central idea: Thinking of something different to do is different and hard work for Zip and Zap.
Sample title: Zip and Zap Do Something Different

Practice 2 (p. 74)
Central idea: Zip and Zap's new moon bicycles are fun to ride.
Sample title: Zip and Zap's New Moon Bicycles

Practice 3 (p. 75)
Central idea: A rich man's plan for quiet is blocked by two carpenters.
Sample title: The Rich Man and the Carpenters

Practice 4 (p. 76)
Central idea: A clever fox outsmarts a cruel lion.
Sample title: The Clever Fox and the Cruel Lion *or* A Fox Outsmarts a Lion

Practice 5 (p. 77)
Central idea: A sad princess can't eat until she has a friend her own age to play with.
Sample title: The Sad Princess *or* The Princess Who Became Thinner and Thinner

Answers to Skill 6
For the student practices in this section, have students reread instructions to check their answers.

Practice 1 (p. 83)
Practice 2 (p. 84)
Practice 3 (p. 85)
Practice 4 (p. 86)

5. 1, 3, 5, 7; 4, 6, 8, 10; O. P. Q. R

Practice 5 (p. 87)
The directions state that you should read the entire list of directions carefully *before doing anything*. You should have done only numbers 6 and 7.

Practice 6 (p. 88)

1. Do nothing. There aren't three triangles.
2. Put the letter *O* in the third circle.
3. Put the number *11* in the first square.
4. Put a circle around all the circles.

Practice 7 (p. 89)

L M N O P Q 7 6 5 4 20 9

1. Do nothing. There aren't more letters than numbers.
2. Put a circle around the second triangle. The numbers 5 + 4 = 9.
3. Put the first letter *L* in the square after the third triangle.
4. Put the number *7* in the third square. There are three odd numbers and three even numbers and 6 + 5 = 11.

Practice 8 (p. 90)

1. cat L M N O P 7 6 5 4 man
2. boy in E F G out fat pan
3.
4.
5.

1. Put a circle around *cat* and *fat*.
2. Put an "X" on *boy*.

3. Put a circle around the letter *F*.
4. Put an "X" above the triangle in the third row.

Practice 9 (p. 91)

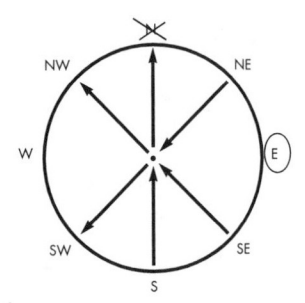

1. Do nothing. There is no arrow pointing *S*, *SE*, *E*, *NE*, and *W*.
2. Do nothing. There is no arrow pointing *S*.
3. Put an "X" on *N*.
4. Put a circle around *E*.

Practice 10 (p. 92)

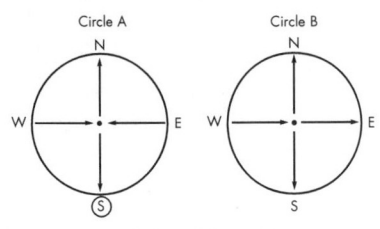

1. Do nothing. There is no arrow pointing *W* in Circle B.
2. Do nothing. The arrows in Circle B are not pointing in four different directions.
3. Put a circle around *S* in Circle A.
4. Do nothing. There is no arrow pointing *W* in Circle B.

Answers to Skill 7

Practice 1 (p. 98)
Children should arrange all vegetables together, all fruits together, and all drinks together. These can be arranged according to pictures or words.

Practice 2 (p. 99)
Children should arrange the animals according to various groups—pets, farm animals, or wild animals. These can be arranged according to pictures or words.

Practice 3 (p. 100)
Children should put the household pictures under the proper headings that have been supplied.

Practice 4 (p. 101)
Children should arrange the shapes into a number of groups. The groups could be as follows: all triangles, all squares, all circles, or all small figures, all medium figures, or all large figures, for example. Some children may be divergent and come up with different kinds of groups. For example: a triangle, square, and a circle; a large square, a medium triangle, a small circle; and so on. These children should be encouraged because the instructions were to group the shapes in as many ways as they can.

Practice 5 (p. 102)
The same as for Practice 4 except that the groups could be as follows: all hearts, all diamonds, all spades, all clubs; all 2's, all 3's, all 4's, all 5's, all 6's, and so on. The children can be divergent and come up with various different kinds of groups.

Practice 6 (p. 103)
Children can arrange the words into a number of different groups. Here are some:

Wild animals: elephant, ape, tiger

Tame animals: all the others

Fowl: hen, drake, gander, goose, turkey, duck

Female animals: hen, sow, mare

Male animals: drake, colt, gander

Pets: colt, mare, puppy, kitten, dog (Many of the other animals can be pets)

Baby animals: puppy, kitten, colt

Farm animals: hen, drake, sow, mare, colt, gander, and so on, except for the elephant, ape, and tiger

Animals: All would be included

Practice 7 (p. 104)
Children can arrange the words into a number of different groups. Here are some:

Things you find in school: Everything would be included

School persons: teacher, principal, nurse, student

Schoolbooks: history books, science books, spelling books

Things for writing: pencil, paper, desk, chalkboard, pen, chalk

© Fearon Teacher Aids FE7965

Rooms in school: classroom, library, auditorium

Games and game equipment: monopoly, baseball, jump rope, basketball, chess, checkers

Indoor games: monopoly, chess, checkers

Outdoor games: baseball, jump rope, basketball

What you find in a classroom: Everything would be included except principal, library, auditorium, nurse

Children may come up with other categories.

Practice 8 (p. 105)
Children can arrange the words into a number of different groups.

Things to wear: Everything would be included

Jewelry: bracelet, earrings, watch

Cold weather clothing: scarf, gloves, sweater, tights, mittens, boots, coat, socks, cap, hat

Girl clothing: dress, stockings, jeans, gown, blouse, skirt, slip, tights, pants (Girls also wear vests and shirts. These, as well as items such as socks, should also be accepted.)

Boy clothing: shirt, vest, jeans, pants. (Items such as socks and caps should also be accepted.)

Footwear: socks, shoes, boots, stockings, tights, slippers

Hand clothing: gloves, mittens

Headwear: cap, hat

Children may come up with other categories.

Practice 9 (p. 106)
1. milk
2. green
3. coat
4. cat
5. circle
6. ten
7. checkers
8. Terry

Practice 10 (p. 107)
1. raisins
2. brown
3. football
4. checkers
5. gloves
6. bathing suit
7. spinach
8. ring

Practice 11 (p. 108)
1. Frank
2. spinach
3. purple
4. door
5. crayon
6. wood
7. ant
8. Susan
9. circle
10. goose

Practice 12 (p. 109)
1. banana
2. twenty
3. seven
4. sixteen
5. princess
6. doe
7. dishwasher
8. eight
9. mustard
10. chalkboard

Practice 13 (p. 110)
1. large
2. pretty
3. pleasant
4. cruel
5. leaf
6. reading
7. cat

Practice 14 (p. 111)
1. vegetables
2. shapes
3. fowl
4. nuts
5. clothing
6. colors
7. names
8. fruits
9. flowers
10. meat

Practice 15 (p. 112)
1. girls' names
2. boys' names
3. bedroom things
4. eating things
5. dried fruit
6. writing things
7. tools
8. food

Practice 16 (p. 113)
1. night
2. July
3. lime
4. fairy tales
5. airplane
6. car
7. twenty-eight (not a multiple of five)
8. United States
9. bull
10. whale (a mammal)

Practice 17 (p. 114)
1. blue
2. pig
3. ice hockey (played on ice)
4. piano
5. two
6. hair (part of the head)
7. hen
8. Europe
9. raisin
10. hoof

Practice 18 (p. 115)
1. duck
2. China
3. right
4. ape
5. mare
6. meat
7. teacher
8. bag
9. beef
10. hat (worn on head rather than body)

Practice 19 (p. 116)
1. seven
2. doe
3. mule
4. tree
5. sugar
6. sock
7. silo
8. pliers (doesn't have a sharp blade)
9. chair
10. fox

Practice 20 (p. 117)
1. Africa
2. eagle
3. long
4. silent
5. mare
6. cabin
7. bell
8. drawer
9. scarf
10. frogs (not a reptile)

Answers to Skill 8
Practice 1 (p. 125)
Example: puppy
1. sad face
2. boy
3. bacon strips
4. queen
5. gasoline pump

Practice 2 (p. 126)
Example: sun
1. thermometer
2. fawn
3. ear
4. branch
5. raincoat

Practice 3 (p. 127)
Example: boat
1. earring
2. money
3. apple
4. prunes

Practice 4 (p. 128)
Example: hat
1. two wheels
2. plane
3. leaf
4. hay

Practice 5 (p. 129)
Example: girl
1. red light
2. branch
3. triangle
4. trunk
5. rain

Practice 6 (p. 130)
Example: carrot
1. ears
2. hands
3. lemon
4. bulb
5. barrel

Practice 7 (p. 131)
Example: beet
1. plane
2. quack
3. finger
4. yellow
5. write

Practice 8 (p. 132)
Example: egg
1. whoo
2. church
3. tame
4. hundred
5. dig

Practice 9 (p. 133)
1. bed
2. smell
3. wolf
4. knee
5. sentence
6. story

Practice 10 (p. 134)
1. stable
2. hot
3. drake
4. sow
5. drink
6. cruel

Practice 11 (p. 135)
1. young
2. bean
3. soft
4. cub
5. doe
6. quiet
7. always
8. weak
9. less
10. yesterday

Practice 12 (p. 136)
1. low
2. toe
3. nephew
4. neigh
5. drake
6. dollar
7. buy
8. empty
9. eat
10. wheel

Practice 13 (p. 137)
1. cold
2. even
3. dumb
4. lemon
5. vehicle

© Fearon Teacher Aids FE7965

6. dollar
7. star
8. clothing
9. silk
10. eight

Practice 14 (p. 138)
1. hangar
2. sister
3. Africa
4. four
5. rough
6. drink
7. excuse
8. shout
9. turtle
10. mildew

Practice 15 (p. 139)
1. clean
2. four
3. Asia
4. country
5. reverend
6. before
7. feet
8. clothing
9. pupil
10. today

Answers to Skill 9
Practice 1 (p. 144)
1. dry—slippery
2. scales—feathers
3. noon—night
4. bead—bread
5. sets—rises

Practice 2 (p. 145)
1. northern—western
2. dawn—dusk
3. crow—cow
4. dimes—quarters
5. bear—beard

Practice 3 (p. 146)
1. tame—wild
2. ducklings—chicks
3. mare—doe
4. salt—sugar
5. thee—three

Practice 4 (p. 147)
1. jungle—farm
2. evening—morning
3. hen—rooster
4. blowing—crowing
5. rooster—hen
6. in—on
7. three—five
8. quiet—noisy

Practice 5 (p. 148)
1. his—her
2. cloudy—sunny
3. moon—sun
4. morning—noon
5. Few—Many
6. low—loud
7. walked—stopped
8. four—three
9. Mr.—Mrs.
10. started—stopped
11. mean—kind

Answers to Skill 10
Practice 1 (p. 153)
1. O
2. O
3. O
4. F
5. F

Practice 2 (p. 154)
1. O
2. F
3. F
4. O
5. O

Practice 3 (p. 155)
1. F
2. O
3. O
4. F
5. F

Practice 4 (p. 156)
1. O
2. O
3. F
4. O
5. F

Practice 5 (p. 157)
1. F
2. O
3. F
4. O
5. O

Answers to Skill 11
Answers to Practices 1–5 may vary.